WRITERS AND CRITICS

Chief Editors
A. NORMAN JEFFARES
R. L. C. LORIMER

Advisory Editors
DAVID DAICHES   C. P. SNOW

645

ORWELL

EDWARD M. THOMAS

OLIVER AND BOYD
EDINBURGH AND LONDON

OLIVER AND BOYD LTD
Tweeddale Court
Edinburgh 1

39A Welbeck Street
London W.1

First published 1965
Reprinted 1968

05 001437 4

Printed in Great Britain by Oliver and Boyd Ltd

CONTENTS

FOR MY MOTHER AND FATHER

ACKNOWLEDGMENTS

For permission to quote from George Orwell's works acknowledgments are due to Martin Secker & Warburg Ltd and to Harcourt, Brace & World, Inc.

The photograph on the front cover is reproduced by permission of Vernon Richards.

E.M.T.

ABBREVIATED TITLES BY WHICH GEORGE ORWELL'S WORKS ARE CITED IN REFERENCES

A.F.	=	*Animal Farm.*
B.D.	=	*Burmese Days.*
C.D.	=	*A Clergyman's Daughter.*
C.E.	=	*Critical Essays.*
C.U.A.	=	*Coming Up for Air.*
D.O.	=	*Down and Out in London and Paris.*
E.Y.E.	=	*England Your England.*
H.T.C.	=	*Homage to Catalonia.*
K.A.F.	=	*Keep the Aspidistra Flying.*
L.A.U.	=	*The Lion and the Unicorn.*
R.W.P.	=	*The Road to Wigan Pier.*
S.A.E.	=	*Shooting an Elephant.*

CHAPTER I

THE MAKING OF AN INDEPENDENT

"He was a virtuous man." This remark, made to Lionel Trilling by a student of his, seems one of the best things ever said about Orwell. It registers honestly and directly what most people feel on reading him—the impact of a moral force. Dr Johnson immediately comes to mind as being the same type of force, something which cannot be contained within the limits of merely literary judgment. Indeed, it is interesting that the adjective "Orwellian" like "Johnsonian," should have passed into the language with the same ambiguity of referring to qualities both of the man and of the work.

In the case of Orwell the two are particularly difficult to disentangle. Beyond the bare dates there is little external evidence for his life—we are not much helped by the fragmentary reminiscences of his friends; his wish that no one should write his biography has been respected. Evidence for his life inside his own works abounds, but it is precisely here that our difficulty arises. The figure we know as Orwell is almost entirely the figure projected in his autobiographical books and essays, which, despite their easy colloquial manner, are far from being spontaneous self-expression. All the books in which Orwell speaks of himself have a serious social or political purpose, and were often re-written several times with regard for the passionate and convincing phrase; and it is therefore probable, perhaps inevitable, that the character presented there as Orwell should be a heightened version, a sharper definition, of the man his friends remember as quieter, more tolerant, and with more sides to his character. Like the stage character who is not presented in every detail, but only in so far as the details are relevant to the dramatic purpose, so the character of Orwell is a series of positions taken up in front of the problems with which he chose to concern himself.

Even the name Orwell was something deliberately assumed; he chose it for himself when his literary character was already comparatively well-formed. He was born Eric Hugh Blair in 1903, in Bengal, where his father was an official in the Customs and Excise. Very soon after he was born the family (but not his father) moved to England. The years before he was sent away to preparatory school were lonely; although devoted to his mother, Orwell felt unable to speak freely to her, while his sisters were too far separated from him in age to be his companions. But already he was reacting to his isolation in a strongly individual way, and from the start this inner independence, his way of asserting himself against the environment, seems to have been connected with the idea of writing:

> From a very early age, perhaps the age of five or six, I knew that when I grew up I should be a writer. . . . I had the lonely child's habit of making up stories and holding conversations with imaginary persons, and I think from the very start my literary ambitions were mixed up with the feelings of being isolated and undervalued. I knew that I had a facility with words and a power of facing unpleasant facts, and I felt that this created a sort of private world in which I could get my own back for my failure in everyday life.[1]

The sense of failure must have been confirmed by his prep-school experience. His account of those years can be found in an essay, "Such, such were the Joys," discovered among Orwell's papers after his death, and still only available in the American edition, because of fears in Britain of possible libel actions. The essay is a compendium of the horrors that might be thought to make a sensitive child suffer at a boarding school. Christopher Hollis, who was with Orwell at Eton, but not at the prep-school, is inclined to think that he exaggerates:[2] but Cyril Connolly, a contemporary at both schools, corroborates much of what Orwell says, especially about the moral blackmail used by the all-powerful wife of the headmaster. And then, of course, Orwell had his own special problems; he was poorer than the other boys and had been accepted at reduced fees because of his academic promise, that is to say, the possibility that he might win the school a scholarship to a good public school. He was repeatedly reminded, sometimes in public, of his dependent position, and reproached for not making the efforts expected from a boy under special obligations to the school. On some occasions he was told that he had already let them down, and that, coming from the social level which he did, he could only hope for a job in a grubby little office.

In a general way it is easy to see this sense of failure at work in Orwell's early novels; indeed, it is arguable that it never left him and that it reasserted itself powerfully in *1984*. His heroes are all isolated figures who resist a hostile society for a time, and try to exist by their own standards, but are then forced to capitulate. Certainly, Orwell never seems to have overcome a tendency to believe that the worst was always bound to happen. These elements have a natural correlation with the suffering of his schooldays; much more difficult to explain is why he should have reacted as he did, by developing a laconic independence and the capacity to strike back effectively. Kipling is an interesting comparison; he, too, suffered bitterly at school, but the result was that he identified himself with the instrument of power. Orwell, from an early age, was to resist authority and to resist it in earnest. "I was a stage rebel, Orwell a true one,"[3] wrote Cyril Connolly, who also records a remark from the prep-school days which is worth repeating because it already seems to have the full flavour of laconic Orwellian independence: "Of course you realise, Connolly, that whoever wins this war, we shall emerge a second rate nation."[4]

Orwell obtained a scholarship to Eton, and in the years that followed held his own in the precocious company of Eton scholars, although he later claimed that from then on he did the minimum of work. After his prep-school, the Eton atmosphere was comparatively congenial, but his subsequent feelings about the school were, as with many other people, ambivalent. Speaking in his last years of the education he would give his adopted son, he is reported to have said that if by the time the boy was of age the public schools still existed, he would like to send him to Eton, but that he hoped that by then they would no longer exist. Nevertheless in few other schools would Orwell's independence have been given room to flourish as it did at Eton.

The next step after Eton would normally have been Oxford or Cambridge, but instead, on leaving, he joined the Indian Imperial Police, and spent the years 1922–7 as a sub-divisional officer in Burma. How this came about is rather obscure. Orwell himself hinted at financial obstacles to a university career, and also mentioned the advice of a master at school. Christopher Hollis discounts any real problem of money, and takes Orwell's decision to go to Burma as evidence of a deep need not to conform. A simpler explanation might be family tradition, since both sides of his family had been connected with the East for several generations. All one can say, perhaps, on the evidence available, is that the decision continued and confirmed the characteristic trajectory of Orwell's development.

The five years of isolation in Burma must have been decisive for his approach to writing; at a formative age he was removed from the world of intellectual discussion and the literary reviews with their quick succession of opinions and ideas, and given instead action and responsibility and the solitude in which to meditate on the injustice to which his work made him a party. He gathered his experience long before he had the opportunity to write about it, or at least to write for publication, for all his accounts of this period were both written and published after his return to Europe. This is perhaps why the individual, often physical, experience, dominates in his writing. It is the source of the arguments he develops, not the mere illustration.

This is well shown in his essay "Shooting an Elephant," where he describes how he was called out one morning to deal with an elephant that had run wild, killing a man. He sends for a rifle to defend himself, but when he eventually catches up with the animal, its attack of must is over and it is quietly pulling up tufts of grass and eating them. Orwell knows that the elephant is now harmless, and much too valuable to be shot out of hand:

> But at that moment I glanced round at the crowd that had followed me. It was an immense crowd, two thousand at the least and growing every minute. It blocked the road for a long distance on either side. I looked at the sea of yellow faces above the garish clothes—faces all happy and excited over this bit of fun, all certain that the elephant was going to be shot. They were watching me as they would watch a conjurer about to perform a trick. They did not like me, but with the magical rifle in my hands I was momentarily worth watching. And suddenly I realised that I should have to shoot the elephant after all. The people expected it of me and I had got to do it; I could feel their two thousand wills pressing me forward irresistibly. And it was at this moment, as I stood there with the rifle in my hands, that I first

grasped the hollowness, the futility of the white man's dominion in the East. Here was I, the white man with his gun, standing in front of the unarmed native crowd—seemingly the leader of the piece; but in reality I was only an absurd puppet pushed to and fro by the will of those yellow faces behind. I perceived in this moment that when the white man turns tyrant it is his own freedom he destroys. He becomes a sort of hollow, posing dummy, the conventionalized figure of a sahib. For it is the condition of his rule that he shall spend his life in trying to impress the 'natives', and so in every crisis he has got to do what the natives expect of him. He wears a mask, and his face grows to fit it.[5]

This effect of realisation dawning on the mind is only possible because Orwell has the talent for descriptive detail which is needed to re-create the physical situation. He was naturally fascinated by odd bits of information and by the variety of things, though perhaps more by their function and mechanics than by colour or surface; so that observation of detail came easily to him, and all the more so because he had practised it from childhood. In "Why I Write," he recalls how between the ages of about ten and twenty-five he had a compulsion to describe things, and carried on a little game with himself:

For minutes at a time this kind of thing would be running through my head: "He pushed the door open and entered the room. A yellow beam of sunlight, filtering through the muslin curtains, slanted on to the table, where a matchbox, half-open, lay beside the inkpot. Down in the street a tortoiseshell cat was chasing a dead leaf," etc. etc.[6]

The careful description of the physical context is what predisposes us to share Orwell's feelings: but these are finally carried over to us only when the documentary style emerges into a strong personal rhetoric. Orwell says nothing about the development of his rhetorical style, but it is fair to assume that this too was studied. Several of his most successful devices can be found in Swift, an author whose techniques he greatly admired. Some of the best moments in his essays are when, after the meticulous description, Orwell's rhetorical conclusion comes home. In the passage quoted above it comes, in a turn of phrase taken directly out of Swift, when he says: "In that moment I perceived . . ."

In his other Burmese essay, "A Hanging," he describes in great detail the scene of a prison execution:

> It was in Burma, a sodden morning of the rains. A sickly light, like yellow tinfoil, was slanting over the high walls into the jail yard. We were waiting outside the condemned cells, a row of sheds fronted with double bars, like small animal cages.[7]

For several paragraphs Orwell recounts how the prisoner is brought out, mentioning the terrible irrelevance of a small dog which has got into the yard and dances round the condemned man. Then comes a passage of minute physical description, building up the tension, which finally breaks when the rhetorical protest, beginning quietly, asserts its strong emotional rhythm:

> It was about forty yards to the gallows. I watched the bare brown back of the prisoner marching in front of me. He walked clumsily with his bound arms, but quite steadily, with that bobbing gait of the Indian who never straightens his knees. At each step his muscles slid neatly into place, the lock of hair on his scalp danced up and down, his feet printed themselves on the wet gravel. And once, in spite of the men who gripped him by each shoulder, he stepped lightly aside to avoid a puddle on the path.
>
> It is curious, but till that moment I had never

realised what it means to destroy a healthy, conscious man. When I saw the prisoner step aside to avoid the puddle I saw the mystery, the unspeakable wrongness, of cutting a life short when it is in full tide. This man was not dying, he was alive just as we are alive. All the organs of his body were working—bowels digesting food, skin renewing itself, nails growing, tissues forming—all toiling away in solemn foolery. His nails would still be growing when he stood on the drop, when he was falling through the air with a tenth of a second to live. His eyes saw the gravel and the grey walls, and his brain still remembered, foresaw, reasoned—even about puddles. He and we were a party of men walking together, seeing, hearing, feeling, understanding the same world; and in two minutes, with a sudden snap, one of us would be gone—one mind less, one world less.

"Shooting an Elephant" and "A Hanging" are among the best essays Orwell ever wrote, and they certainly provide the most classic examples of his method of progressing from the individual experience to the general conclusion. Yet is is difficult to fix their precise excellence; it is not enough to say that his sentiments are honourable, for hatred of oppression and sympathy for the oppressed do not in themselves make for memorable prose; they are the strongest Orwellian characteristics, perhaps, but they are not the distinguishing ones. What *is* distinctive is his ability to record on the page the progress of a creative intelligence, producing ideas not from the ideas of others, but from the experience of life itself.

Burmese Days, written when he was back in Europe but projected much earlier, is Orwell's only novel to draw on his experience in the East. He later suggested that it was written as a necessary exorcism, and certainly it is predominantly, though not entirely, a painful book.

Unlike the essays it is written entirely from inside the situation, though not in the first person. There is no one to draw Orwellian conclusions, for Flory, the hero, like Orwell's later heroes, is Orwell without his quality of moral courage—perhaps one could say without his dimension of writer, since this was the role in which he most often chose to oppose injustice.

Flory is an English timber-merchant, one of the small white community which revolves round the European Club at Kyauktada in Upper Burma. At thirty-five he is the victim of the isolation of his life, which has undermined his will without destroying his capacity for self-criticism, He is lazy, drunken, bored by his Burmese mistress, and driven to desperation by the *pukka-sahib* talk of the club. His only friend is the local doctor, Veraswami, an Indian, who is much more pro-British than Flory is. Yet when it is suggested, as a matter of Government policy, that clubs should admit at least one non-white member, Flory lacks the courage to back his friend. The suggestion seems to be that at the root of Flory's moral cowardice lies, not a desire to conform, but a sense of guilt. This is symbolised by a disfiguring birthmark on the left cheek, which in company he manoeuvres to keep out of sight. As far as is known, Orwell himself had no physical defect, though he certainly says that at school he imagined himself ugly, and considered that other people must be revolted by him. His contemporaries there deny that he was ever thought of as anything other than rather distinguished in appearance, and the likelihood seems to be that his sense of failure was projected in physical terms.

The central theme of the book is how hope and courage are reborn in Flory with the arrival in the community of Elizabeth Lackersteen, a young woman come from England to visit her aunt and uncle. Flory's hopes come to nothing and the book ends with his despair and suicide. The chief criticism one can make of the book is that the fall of Flory depends too much on events that are external and coincidental. Thus at the very moment when he is about to propose marriage, an earthquake occurs. It is a pity that Orwell should have relied so heavily on external factors, because in places he makes us aware of the underlying incompatibility of Elizabeth and Flory, which they can never see because they want to believe differently, Flory projects on to her all his yearnings for intellectual companionship. She has been living for the last few years in Paris with her "artistic" widowed mother, and this association with the symbolic city of culture counts for more in his mind than the fact that they never manage to converse easily about anything except trivial things.

For Elizabeth, the life in Paris is something squalid which she wants to forget. Unlike Flory she finds the life of the European Club attractive; it reminds her of her own family's way of life before her father's bankruptcy and death, and her mother's move to Paris. Here Orwell hints at the relationship between class divisions at home and oppression abroad which he was later to discuss in terms of his own family background. When she first arrived in Kyauktada, Elizabeth thought: "it was almost like being really rich, the way people lived in India." If she cannot marry someone during her stay with her aunt (and there are very few eligible men), she faces the prospect of having to earn her living back in England. Thus, although several things displease and even repel her in Flory, particularly his interest in the ways of the Burmese, she has an underlying need to discount these feelings about the only suitor; and there are moments, when the conversation turns on guns and hunting, when she can really admire him. Indeed the only successful event in their relationship is a hunting expedition. The tense physical excitement which Orwell is able to convey in his description shows the attraction which this type of active life held, not only for Elizabeth Lackersteen but for himself:

> Ten yards away a little cock the size of a bantam was pecking vigorously at the ground. He was beautiful, with his long silky neck-feathers, bunched comb and arching, laurel-green tail. There were six hens with him, smaller brown birds, with diamond-shaped feathers like snake-scales on their backs. All this Elizabeth and Flory saw in the space of a second, then with a squak and a whirr the birds were up and flying like bullets for the jungle. Instantly, automatically as it seemed, Elizabeth raised her gun and fired. It was one of those shots where there is no aiming, no consciousness of the gun in one's hand, when one's mind seems to fly behind the charge and drive it to the mark. She knew the bird was doomed even before she pulled the trigger, He tumbled, showering feathers thirty yards away.[8]

This brings us to a point about Orwell (or is it a charge against him?) made by Malcolm Muggeridge[9] "that there was a Kiplingesque as well as a rebel side to his character." There is evidence in *Burmese Days* apart from the hunting expedition, to support this view, particularly an incident, told in true boys' adventure-story fashion, in which Flory rescues the European community besieged in their club by hostile Burmese. Again, there is perhaps a note of grudging admiration in the descriptions of Verrall, an arrogant military police officer whose aristocratic self-confidence humiliates Flory and captivates Elizabeth. Most readers of *Burmese Days* will agree that it is not unfair to collect these aspects of the book under the heading "Kiplingesque." There was certainly something in Orwell which responded to the active life, the feel of guns, the excitement of hunting, something which admired physical bravery, the capacity to make decisions and to accept responsibility. He once made a list of his favourite short stories, and, as was pointed out, they could all be described as action-stories. What has to be established is the relation of this side of him to the angry, anti-imperialist side. Is the conclusion to be that, below the level of the conscious mind, he approved of empires and armies, and the upper-class tradition of service and authority which was their mainstay and into which he was born; in fact that he was secretly of the devil's party? A similar charge was made by Victor Gollancz in a different context when disagreeing with Orwell's views on the English class system: "Mr Orwell is still a victim of that early atmosphere in his home and public school."

In the case of a novel which succeeds, as *Burmese Days* does, in being a novel and not a tract, it is difficult either to refute or to sustain such an interpretation finally. Although Orwell clearly disapproves of British domination in Burma, the novel does not give the impression that it was written merely to express this disapproval. Even Ellis, the most ferocious native-hater of all the Europeans who gather in the club, is too real and terrible in his venom to be a conventional representative of white imperialism, while the brooding figure of U Po Kyin, the completely amoral Burmese magistrate, makes one realise that there will not necessarily be an end of oppression with the departure of the British. The fact that Orwell is not in pamphleteering mood in *Burmese Days* proves no more than that he had some of that capacity for inclusive sympathy which is usually admired in a novelist.

It is fortunate that outside the novel Orwell has given explicit consideration to this question of the "Kiplingesque" virtues. In his essay on Kipling he faces the fact that while he abhors many of Kipling's attitudes, he nevertheless enjoys reading him. He finds that he cannot support T. S. Eliot's apologia for Kipling, and insists

Kipling *is* a jingo imperialist, he *is* morally indefensible and aesthetically disgusting. It is better to start by admitting that, and then to try to find out why it is that he survives while the refined people who have sniggered at him wear so badly.[10]

One reason, Orwell finds, is that Kipling had a grip on reality. Because he identified himself with the official class, he possessed "one thing which enlightened people seldom or never possess, and that is a sense of responsibliity." Orwell, too, knew what responsibility meant. Although he dissociated himself from the attitudes and customs of the Europeans in Burma, he had shared their life and knew that it was not an easy one.

Besides you could forgive the Europeans a great deal of their bitterness. Living and working among orientals would try the patience of a saint. And all of them, the officials particularly, knew what it was to be baited and insulted.[11]

Orwell could not wholly turn against and vilify the tradition of "service," because he knew from his own upbringing and his family's connexion with the Empire, that there was a species of idealism mixed in with the hypocrisy and stupidity. When he felt that this tradition was being attacked irresponsibly he reacted sharply in its defence, as he did in 1940:

It is all very well to be "advanced" and "enlightened," to snigger at Colonel Blimp and proclaim your emancipation from all traditional loyalties, but a time comes when the sand of the desert is sodden red and what have I done for thee England my England? As I was brought up in this tradition myself I can recognize it under strange disguises, and also sympathise with it, for even at its stupidest and most sentimental it is a comelier thing than the shallow self-righteousness of the left-wing intelligentsia.[12]

If there are any contradictions in Orwell's wide sympathies they are held in suspension in his novel. Where he chose a more discursive form, he resolved them. It is dangerous to attribute unconscious motives to Orwell, since he himself was always investigating his own attitudes in search of them. His method was to admit contradictory and even disreputable emotions in himself, and then to judge between them. He has left us in no doubt that his judgment on British rule in Burma was that it was indefensible, and his pronouncement is all the more convincing because it is not hysterical and not made easily. "In order to hate imperialism you have got to be part of it."[13]

What Orwell wrote about Burma seems more mature and effective than his other early work, and this may be because the issues there were comparatively clear-cut and his own experience far enough away by the time he came to write about it. His next themes, class and poverty, were ones he could not get away from, but had to write about as he struggled with them in his own life. Yet though the writings about Burma stand apart, the years spent there were largely responsible for deciding the later course of his life. Orwell tells us that it was reaction against his work as an agent of oppression which made him from then on wish to identify himself with the oppressed wherever he found them. And perhaps there was another, less obvious way in which Burma formed him: it confirmed him as the outsider, the man who could look at England as a whole, and it confirmed his sense of responsibility. Although he abandoned and attacked the traditional and conventional idols of his country, he created instead his own ideal of England, and for this he was ready to die; so that with all his loyalties redefined, Orwell is still the lonely figure defending the outposts, the legionary standing guard on the wall.

REFERENCES

1. *E.Y.E.*, p. 7.
2. Christopher Hollis, *George Orwell*, 1956, pp. 2–4.
3. Cyril Connolly, *Enemies of Promise*, 1961, p. 178.
4. *Enemies of Promise*, p. 179.
5. *S.A.E.*, p. 6.
6. *E.Y.E.*, p. 8.
7. *S.A.E.*, p. 11.
8. *B.D.*, p. 167.
9. *World Review*, Jun. 1950.
10. *C.E.*, p. 112.
11. *B.D.*, p. 34.
12. "The Limit to Pessimism," in *New English Weekly*, 25 Apr. 1940.
13. *R.W.P.*, p. 145.

CHAPTER II

POVERTY

Burmese Days was not Orwell's first published book. *Down and Out in Paris and London* preceded it by two years, and is a rearranged but substantially true autobiographical account of some months in the summer and autumn of 1929. Before the book begins Orwell has been living for eighteen months in a cheap Paris boarding-house where he must have gone soon after his return from Burma. He had saved some money and wanted to devote himself to writing. It may be that he also had some idea of taking up the French strand in his ancestry, for his mother's father was a Frenchman who went out to Burma.

The book starts as his money is running out, and when his remaining cash is stolen, he is forced to find a job or starve. Since it is a time of unemployment he comes very near to starving before he eventually finds work as a dishwasher in the subterranean world of dirt, sweat, and curses which supports the carpeted elegance of an expensive restaurant. His power of observation makes this part of the book fascinating, and his descriptions alternate easily with perceptive comment. Here he is discussing the outlook of a waiter in an expensive restaurant:

> His work gives him the mentality, not of a workman but of a snob. He lives perpetually in sight of rich people, stands at their tables, listens to their conversations, sucks up to them with smiles and discreet little jokes. He has the pleasure of spending money by proxy.[1]

Orwell is a good model for the concerned or "committed" writer, but one has to recognise that this style and method *is* imitable. The alternation of concrete detail with sociological comment has become the stock-in-trade of a certain sort of left-wing writing. Cyril Connolly once jumbled up sentences from three passages of typical documentary of this sort, one of them by Orwell, and demonstrated that the styles were indistinguishable. Taken over a short stretch this method of criticism is not so unfair as it seems. If you open almost any page of *Down and Out* or *The Road to Wigan Pier* you find a serviceable and economical but scarcely distinctive style.

Taken as a whole, however, the first of these books is remarkable for never falling into falsity or irrelevance, which are perhaps the special dangers for this sort of writing. Orwell is writing not merely about the situation, but from within it. He is involved in the life he describes in the way one can only be involved in one's own life. This comes out in the irreducible individual note which is the lyric phrase:

> It was strange coming up into the street from those firelit cellars. The air seemed blindingly clear and cold, like arctic summer, and how sweet the petrol did smell after the stench of sweat and food.[2]

or again:

> There was—it is hard to express it—a sort of heavy contentment, the contentment a well-fed beast might feel, in a life which had become so simple.[3]

This identification of himself with the life he is describing can further be seen in such a small thing as his use of the inclusive "we," or in his frequent repetition that he is giving this account of things not out of curiosity or love of the picaresque, but because it is the truth:

> I am trying to describe the people in our quarter,

> not for the mere curiosity, but because they are all part of the story. Poverty is what I am writing about, and I had my first contact with poverty in this slum. The slum, with its dirt and its queer lives, was first an object-lesson in poverty, and then the background for my own experiences. It is for that reason that I try to give some idea of what life was like there.[4]

Despite the hardship of life there, the part of the book which deals with his experiences in France has vitality, even gaiety. The company on Saturday nights in his local *bistro* clearly remained a good memory for Orwell. By contrast, the section of the book which deals with England has an atmosphere of unrelieved depression. This reflects what is no doubt in part a real difference between poverty on wine in the communal atmosphere of the Paris slum, and poverty on "tea and two slices" as a tramp in empty London suburbs. But more important than this, the return to England brought Orwell to a poverty which was interwoven with the class structure he knew from childhood; the second part of the book is so much more painful because humiliation is here added to hardship. He has to fight not only against the physical circumstances of poverty but also against his own inbred middle-class feelings of status and self-respect.

When Orwell arrives in London he finds that a promised job is not immediately available, and decides to go on the road. What follows is a grey life of insult in casual wards, queueing for charitable cups of tea in church halls, life on tea and bread and marge, undernourishment sapping the strength and the will. With the exception of Bozo, the pavement artist, the characters he meets in England are colourless and undifferentiated; indeed, the main point that Orwell is concerned to make is that poverty is not merely an inconvenient absence of material comforts, but a real degradation of the character:

> Hunger reduces one to an utterly spineless, brainless condition, more like the after-effects of influenza than anything else. It is as though one had been turned into a jelly-fish, or as though all one's blood had been pumped out and luke-warm water substituted.[5]

As yet Orwell makes no political formulation, but he already faces in this direction. His concrete proposals are limited to a plan for providing work for tramps in market-gardens, but when he asks what it is that makes the nation ready to tolerate the misery of large numbers of unemployed, roaming the country in search of work, he hits upon the interrelated themes of injustice and class-feeling which were to lead him, in the pages of *The Road to Wigan Pier*, to his own individualistic socialism. In *Down and Out* he is content merely to ask the question and to set down the truth about a kind of life which is remote from the experience of most readers. This objective purpose of Orwell's should be kept in mind, if only to counterbalance the attention that has been given to his personal motivation. *Why* Orwell went down and out is a question that has fascinated his friends and critics, perhaps beyond its real relevance to his writing, but it is something which must be discussed briefly.

At the beginning of *Down and Out*, the poverty of the narrator is shown to be the natural result of external necessity. In fact, of course, Orwell had friends to whom he could send for money to get out of France, and to whom he could appeal for a job in England. John Wain finds an evasive streak in the book, due to this factor.[6] The gulf between the inhabitants of the Paris slum and the narrator, who can without too great difficulty, have enough money sent to buy himself a railway ticket home, is not explored. This would not matter so much if it were better concealed, that is, if the account were made more fictitious, but as it is there are moments of uneasiness for the reader when the narrator eventually just walks out of the two worlds of poverty, first in Paris and then in England.

To explore the gulf would have meant confronting the deep internal compulsion to identify himself with poverty and suffering, and this he was not yet ready to do. Later, in *The Road to Wigan Pier*, he describes his feelings at the time he returned from Burma, and speaks of expiating an immense weight of guilt. His opposition to imperialist oppression had, he says, led him to associate himself with the underdog everywhere, to identify himself always with the victim, to make a virtue of failure. He adopted in everything an exaggerated position, seeking out the extremes of poverty among what his family would have called "the lowest of the low." It is difficult to believe that Burma is the whole explanation, especially when one reads his next two books, *A Clergyman's Daughter* and *Keep the Aspidistra Flying*. These show clearly that his rejection of the respectable world is bound up with class feeling, and his own early background and schooling. Here we must look more closely at the family in which he was brought up, or rather, the type of family, for although Orwell was always making oblique references to his background, he seldom spoke specifically of his parents. He has several descriptions of Anglo-Indian families living back in England in "reduced circumstances," and it is not improbable that his own was at least partly the model:

> People in this class owned no land, but they felt that they were landowners in the sight of God, and kept up a semi-aristocratic outlook by going into the professions and the fighting services rather than into trade. Small boys used to count the plum stones on

> their plates and foretell their destiny by chanting "Army, Navy, Church, Medicine, Law"; and even of these "Medicine" was faintly inferior to the others and only put in for the sake of symmetry. To belong to this class when you were at the £400 a year level was a queer business, for it meant that your gentility was almost purely theoretical. You lived, so to speak, at two levels simultaneously. Theoretically you knew all about servants and how to tip them, although in practice you had one, or, at most, two resident servants. Theoretically you knew how to wear your clothes and how to order a dinner, although in practice you could never afford to go to a decent tailor or a decent restaurant.[7]

What Orwell stressed was the colourlessness of this straining, gentlemanly poverty, where vitality had been killed by worry, and even a glass of beer was a reckless extravagance. Hilda, wife of the hero in a later book of his, comes from just such a family, and this is how her husband describes her:

> What Hilda lacks—I discovered this about a week after we were married—is any kind of joy in life, any interest in things for their own sake. The idea of doing things because you enjoy them is something she can hardly understand.[8]

It is hard to say how far in these passages Orwell may have exaggerated the drabness of his own family background. Some who knew the family have protested that they were much less dreary than the characters of Orwell's novels. But it is interesting that in every novel greyness is the ordinary condition in which life is lived. There are occasional glimpses of beauty, usually associated with the countryside, but his heroes live in the suburbs; however far their thoughts may range, it is assumed that the reality is the alarm-clock ringing in the grey dawn for another day of work.

Working-class life, when not twisted by unemployment, seemed by contrast colourful to Orwell. Here was a less neurotic way of living, where people at least spent their money on enjoying themselves, not on keeping up appearances. Yet he found the approach to the working class difficult. The corollary of the penurious gentility was an exaggerated contempt for "commonness," which could not be overcome by merely taking thought. The economic margin between the bottom of the "gentlemanly" class and the top of the trading and working classes was so narrow, and the social distinction the former aimed to preserve so great, that, as in the attitudes of poor whites to negroes, contempt was the index of their fears. Involuntarily, Orwell shared the loathing for the "commonness" and dirtiness which he was brought up to believe were inseparable from working people. Indeed his feelings were aggravated by an unusual capacity for physical revulsion.

The combination of home and school background, the sense of failure, and wish to get away from his own class, and an ambiguous attitude to the poor, offer a coherent explanation of a great deal in Orwell's earlier books. Burma is not a separate or irrelevant experience; it was the tradition of his childhood, of "character-building" and "taking responsibility," which had sent him to be an agent of colonial oppression. He was now cutting himself away not merely from the work of policeman in Burma but from the whole tradition which made that work possible; and he was doing it with the thoroughness and dedication of that tradition at its best. He wanted to sink below all the standards of his background, and thus remove all the inbuilt anxieties about conforming to them.

In *The Road to Wigan Pier* he describes his own feelings on first entering the underworld of London poverty. He sets out one day and finds himself a common lodging-house in Limehouse Causeway. The place had the same error for him, he says, "as a sewer full of rats." The 'Deputy" who collects his ninepence ignores his .ccent (Orwell had been worried that this would mark im out), and shows him into the kitchen. There follows vhat must have been a great moment for Orwell:

There were stevedores and navvies and a few sailors sitting about and playing draughts and drinking tea. They barely glanced at me as I entered. But this was Saturday night and a hefty young stevedore was drunk and was reeling about the room. He turned, saw me and lurched towards me with broad red face thrust out and a dangerous-looking fishy gleam in his eyes. I stiffened myself. So the fight was coming already. The next moment the stevedore collapsed on my chest and flung his arms round my neck. " 'Ave a cup of tea, chum" he cried tearfully; " 'Ave a cup of tea."[9]

Symptomatic of the rejection of his background was he change from Eric Blair to George Orwell. He never vent so far as to change his name by deed poll, but the ransformation was certainly something more than is isually implied by taking a *nom de plume*. As late as)ecember 1934 he signed himself "Eric Blair" below an rticle in *The Adelphi*, but "George Orwell" had already ppeared on his first published book, and it became more nd more the name he used when writing private letters o his friends. Orwell told T. R. Fyvel that he didn't ke Eric because of associations with romantic Norse eroes in school stories. Blair was a Scots name, and here he associations seem to have been with the grouse noors and deer-forests which had been the boast of he richer boys at his prep-school every year as the ummer came round. The hero of *Keep the Aspidistra 'lying* has a Scottish Christian name, Gordon, and eplores it, along with the other gifts of Scotland to the world—"golf, whisky, porridge, and the works of Barri and Stevenson."

It is hard to know how seriously to take this curiou prejudice. Clearly it was more than whimsical, an suggests that he wanted to forget his Scottish ancestr and his education. On the other hand it is too slight thing to bear the weight of involved interpretation. I the end Orwell *did* go to live in Scotland. However what is undeniable is that the new name (the patro saint plus an English river) expressed admirably th robust Englishness of the *persona* he now created fo himself. Yet before this really crystallised there cam two rather painful books in which he worked out som of the conflicts in his background—*A Clergyman's Daughte* (1935), and *Keep the Aspidistra Flying* (1936).

The theme of the first book is a rather unlikely on for Orwell—religious faith and the state when faith ha been lost, the completeness of each state to itself and th impossibility of explaining the transition. The plo seems, at first sight, well-suited to the theme, since th two states are separated by the loss of memory of th chief character, Dorothy. She is the daughter of a selfish widowed rector, harassed by tradesman's debts, over working herself in Church activities. She is still fairl young, though clearly headed for spinsterhood, whe she loses her memory and finds herself penniless i London. First she falls in with a group of Cockne youths going to work in the hop-fields; later, when he memory has returned but she is still prevented from goin home by local scandal about her disappearance, sh lives, as Orwell had done, among the destitute c London. One chapter is the sustained account in wha is, for Orwell, rather adventurous semi-dramatic forr of a night Dorothy spends in Trafalgar Square, wrappe in newspapers, and huddling together with the othe homeless wanderers of the city.

Dorothy now finds that in the process of sinking t

the bottom of society, her religious faith has, inexplicably, gone. After a period spent teaching she is able to return home, where she takes up the daily round of her old duties for its own sake: "The problem of faith and no faith had utterly vanished from her mind."

It is hardly a satisfying conclusion, nor really a satisfying book; in fact it is the only one of his books which Orwell would have liked to suppress—he even went round buying up such copies as he was later able to find. In the first place it is difficult to feel that the question of faith is at all urgent for Orwell, and in addition to this, or perhaps because of it, the various episodes do not form themselves into any pattern. This does not mean that they are not sometimes memorable in themselves. After his days of tramping, Orwell had gathered varied experience as a private schoolmaster and bookshop assistant, as well as in other jobs which he does not mention specifically. He draws on his teaching experience in a comic yet horrifying account of a suburban private school where Dorothy teaches for a while. Again, the book has an excellent evocation of the hop-fields—the physical activity, the exhausted sleep in the straw, the gypsies, and the popular songs on everyone's lips:

> As much part of the atmosphere of the hopfields as the bitter scent and the blowsy sunlight were the tunes of those two songs ringing through the leafy lanes of the bines.[10]

But very soon Orwell is sure to intrude some bare comment of his own, like this:

> Altogether, the farmers had the pickers in a cleft stick; but it was not the farmers who were to blame—the low price of the hops was the root of the trouble.[11]

It is as if Orwell had forgotten what sort of book he was writing. Remarks like this are part of the strength of

Down and Out or *The Road to Wigan Pier* because of the factual context and the autobiographical method. There he can alternate between the record of his experience and the conclusions he draws from it; that is, he can exercise a kind of intellectual control over the experience. In the novel we are considering, the chief character has the same physical and emotional contact with poverty as Orwell had, but being inside the situation and without the formulating capacity of the documentary writer, she remains the sum of the rather disconnected episodes in which she is involved. Most of Orwell's books can justly be called episodic, but in the autobiographical ones the episodes are organised by his conclusions.

Much the same criticisms can be made of *Keep the Aspidistra Flying*. Here the hero, Gordon Comstock, like Orwell, has declared war on all kinds of success. He gives up a job "with good prospects" in an advertising agency and sinks lower and lower in the social scale, ending up as the assistant in a seedy penny-library. But having decided to abandon the respect of others and his own middle-class self-respect, he finds that these things, and even money itself, are somehow bound up with other values in life, He watches the neck of a rich young man browsing in a bookshop and thinks

> You can't have a skin like that under 500 a year. A sort of charm, he had, a glamour like all moneyed people. Money and charm; who shall separate them?[12]

An excursion to the country with his girl, Rosemary, is ruined by lack of money. He overspends on lunch, and all afternoon feels the humiliation of having to get home on her money. (Orwell was very pleased when, after the book's publication, he received letters from young men who claimed he had set down exactly what had happened to them.) Not only is Gordon's relationship with Rosemary undermined, but a friendship with the rich owner-editor of a left-wing review is falsified by the money barrier. The situation embarrasses the one and embitters the other, and illustrates what Orwell elsewhere emphasised, that money and class differences cannot be overcome merely by deciding to ignore their existence.

After sinking beneath respectable society and rejecting everyone, including Rosemary, Gordon recants completely when he finds that she is pregnant by him. He decides to marry, and is to take up his old job in advertising. His literary talents will be employed in persuading people that they suffer from "pedic perspiration." We last see him and Rosemary enjoying the prospect of their cosy flat with breakfast together and furniture on the never-never, and the thought of the child that is coming. It is not clear whether we are to conclude that the rejection of money and success leads ultimately to the rejection of ordinary human feelings.

The book is painful and aggravating to read since it is the almost unbroken expression of self-pity. Indeed, together with *A Clergyman's Daughter* it forms the best evidence for what might be called the "psychological" interpretation of Orwell's work. Because he chose to write in personal and often rhetorical terms he has been presented as a man of neuroses, giving violent and obsessed expression to the traumas of his early life, and these two novels certainly have an atmosphere of enclosed, unrelieved unhappiness which may indicate that the act of writing them was a type of therapeutics. But against this we have to set the fact that Orwell's directly autobiographical writing is by no means oppressive. Furthermore, if we take the period 1931–6, which saw the publication of his three early novels, we find that the same years produced works of a very different tone—*Down and Out*, "A Hanging," and "Shooting an Elephant." Finally, Sir Richard Rees, a friend of his from those days, and perhaps, in part the model for the left-wing editor in *Keep the Aspidistra Flying*, remembers his invariable charm and dry humour in those years.

Perhaps the most satisfying explanation of the difference in quality between Orwell's earlier works is this, that he did not really have the temperament of a novelist, and in trying to write novels was the victim of the dominant literary form of our time. (His later successes were hybrid forms.) He had a talent for the evocation of a mood and for the extraction from that mood of an intellectual argument. The conclusions which he drew were his way of controlling the material. In the other type of control, where the novelist keeps in the background and suggests his meaning by the way he organises the plot, Orwell seems to be lacking. If we compare even his best constructed novel, *Burmese Days*, with another book of similar background, *A Passage to India*, we immediately see that there is none of that delicate arrangement of coincidence and circumstantial irony by which Forster succeeds in suggesting an "order" or meaning in the events he describes. To do this it may be necessary to have some sort of sensed *weltanschauung*, and Orwell's concentration on isolated and contradictory facts precluded this. If there is such a thing as "poetic truth" as distinct from everyday fact, then Orwell only very rarely glimpsed it, which is perhaps why his rather bleak poems seldom catch fire.

The thesis is this: that the novel-form invited Orwell to express his strong emotions without giving him the opportunity he needed to comment on them explicitly. It must be a tentative thesis, but at least it allows not only for his early failures in novel-writing, but also for his early successes in other forms; while the too common view of Orwell as a neurotic spilling over into print, though sufficient to explain him at his worst, must leave us bewildered by the maturity of some of his early work.

REFERENCES

1. *D.O.*, p. 76.
2. *D.O.*, p. 64.
3. *D.O.*, p. 91.
4. *D.O.*, p. 9.
5. *D.O.*, p. 38.
6. John Wain, *Essays on Literature and Ideas*, 1963, p. 201.
7. *R.W.P.*, p. 125.
8. *C.U.A.*, p. 139.
9. *R.W.P.*, p. 153.
10. *C.D.*, p. 128.
11. *C.D.*, p. 132.
12. *K.A.F.*, p. 20.

CHAPTER III

ORWELLIAN SOCIALISM

By 1936 Orwell was living in Hertfordshire. He had recently married and was now keeping a small village store, while at the same time he persevered with articles and book reviews. Then Victor Gollancz, who had published his earlier novels, commissioned him, on behalf of the Left Book Club, to tour the unemployed areas of the north of England, and to write about conditions there. The result was *The Road to Wigan Pier*, written at speed and dealing to a considerable extent with problems that are no longer there, but for all that one of the few readable books of its kind left over from the nineteen-thirties.

Its freshness is no doubt closely connected with its unorthodoxy. Certainly the book which the selectors received cannot have been what they expected, for in an embarrassed Preface, Victor Gollancz felt bound to express his strong disagreement with almost every one of Orwell's main points. But by the time of publication the author was already in Spain, enlisting in the popular militias, and beyond the reach of argument.

The first part of the book is a straight account, with tables of prices and wages, of the physical and psychological effects of unemployment in an industrial area, as Orwell saw them while staying in squalid lodging-houses and visiting people in their homes. On one occasion he went down a mine, and his account of this, collected separately among his essays, has become justly famous. The effect there, and throughout this descriptive section, is achieved by the accumulation of detail and cannot be illustrated fairly by short quotation, but what can be shown are some of his rhetorical conclusions, provided we remember that they follow long pages of painstakingly recorded experience. Thus on the day he finds a full chamber pot under the breakfast-table, Orwell decides to leave the lodging-house where he is staying:

> In the end Mrs Brooker's self-pitying talk—always the same complaints over and over, and always ending with the tremulous whine of "It does seem 'ard, don't it now?"—revolted me even more than her habit of wiping her mouth with bits of newspaper. But it is no use saying that people like the Brookers are disgusting and trying to put them out of mind. For they exist in tens and hundreds of thousands; they are one of the characteristic by-products of the modern world. You cannot disregard them if you accept the civilisation that produced them. For this is part at least of what industrialism has done for us. Columbus sailed the Atlantic, the first steam engine tottered into motion, the British square stood firm under the French guns at Waterloo, the one-eyed scoundrels of the nineteenth century praised God and filled their pockets; and this is where it all led—to labyrinthine slums and dark back kitchens with sickly, ageing people creeping round and round them like blackbeetles. It is a kind of duty to see and smell such places now and again, especially smell them, lest you forget that they exist; though perhaps it is better not to stay there too long.[1]

Orwell's completely undoctrinaire approach to the situations he described, and the independence of his conclusions, made him an awkward ally. He could not refrain from pointing out, for example, that the theoretical socialist, like the capitalist, expected coal to turn up in sacks when he wanted it, and was every bit as remote from the hot underground world of the miner:

> In a way it is humiliating to watch coal-miners working. It raises in you a momentary doubt about your own status as an "intellectual" and a superior person generally. For it is brought home to you, at least while you are watching, that it is only because miners sweat their guts out that superior persons can remain superior. You and I and the editor of the *Times Lit. Supp.*, and the Nancy poets and the Archbishop of Canterbury and Comrade X, author of *Marxism for Infants*—all of us *really* owe the comparative decency of our lives to poor drudges underground, blackened to the eyes, with their throats full of coal dust, driving their shovels forward with arms and belly muscles of steel.[2]

This showed the way the argument was to go in the second half of the book. Beginning with straight autobiography, it ends with sustained criticism of English Socialism and Socialists. The reason Orwell gives for bringing in so much of his own life is that the personal approach is essential: poverty and large-scale unemployment are only tolerated because we are divided by the class-system, and the class-system is something which cannot be discussed in jargon terms but must be seen from within. Orwell claims to be "sufficiently typical of my class, or rather sub-caste, to have a symptomatic importance."

Against this it can be objected that, coming from an Anglo-Indian family, Orwell was by no means typical: but this overlooks the fact that what he is claiming is not that the class feelings of his background are universal in the middle class, but that they show, perhaps in aggravated form, the type of deep irrationalism that lies beneath even moderate class attitudes. In other words, that the exacerbated prejudices of the shock-absorbers of the class system, the people he called the "lower-upper-middle class," are in fact relevant to the generality of people in the same way as abnormal psychology is relevant to the normal. The final test, of course, is whether Orwell's autobiographical remarks and the conclusions he draws, illuminate the subject or not: but about this there is disagreement.

The Road to Wigan Pier is a book which has been attacked savagely, and not only by people who are themselves the objects of Orwell's attacks. Even sympathetic critics and personal friends have called it his worst book. If one does not agree with this judgment, one is bound to look for some explanation of the annoyed reaction the book has generated among so many people. It is very probable that at the root of much of this antipathy lies shock at the violence of some of Orwell's statements, in particular one that has been much-quoted. He says that when he was a child, he quite commonly heard said what people would now be very chary of saying: "The lower classes smell." He then repeats the phrase, and it does seem that he is getting some pleasure from rubbing in to the reader a fact which *he* is willing to face, but which he suspects the reader is not. Taken together with the other evidence for Orwell's acute sense of smell and natural squeamishness (and there is plenty in *Wigan Pier* alone) we are led very soon to the comparison with Swift and the adjective *pathological*. The instance cited is extreme, and in so far as it not only shocks but also antagonises the reader, is a mistake in what aims to be a piece of persuasive writing. But to judge the whole book by such an instance is also a mistake. However extreme and violent the instance of class prejudice he gives, it still illustrates his argument, for it is the *kind* of belief that underlies class attitudes—something taken in imperceptibly during one's upbringing and too deep-set to be removed by an intellectual allegiance to socialist ideology. The case Orwell is making out is in fact far from being hysterical or irresponsible. He is insisting on the depth of class divisions and the difficulty of overcoming them. He also suggests that good and bad is mixed in class attitudes in a manner not easy to disentangle. The Old School Tie mentality should not be sneered at too automatically, for, with all its shortcomings. it includes loyalties which can be useful to the proletariat; and the middle-class Englishman, whether he considers himself a Communist or not, will not find it too easy to think of the working-man as his equal. The moral Orwell draws is that the solution to the class problem is a slow one, of necessity. The best one can do is to have patience and be conscious of the strength of one's own prejudices.

These are sane and comprehensive conclusions. He wants not the victory of one section of the community, but rather the total readjustment of an organic body—the English nation. Seen in the light of his conclusions, the emotional passages in *The Road to Wigan Pier*, though less well-judged than in his later writings, are not irresponsible attacks on more or less arbitrary targets, but rhetoric applied to a strong, intelligent argument.

Orwell's criticism of English Socialism is worth summarising, even though some of the points have lost their relevance, because of the root attitudes and assumptions which he reveals. In the first place he was against dogmatism, against a rigid Marxist analysis of the class system as he knew it in England. Orwell's plain manner might suggest that he was ignorant of the full complexity possible in a Marxist analysis but according to Sir Richard Rees he astonished a Marxist summer school in 1936 by his mastery of the method, and this is not hard to believe after reading *Animal Farm*. Orwell's disagreement with the Marxists was that their picture of England did not tally with his own experience. What is more, he considered that their manner antagonised large sections of the population who were potential supporters of socialism; he felt that the typical contempt for patriotism, genteel accents, and *bourgeois* manners obscured the real economic divisions, and that, faced with an ideological struggle presented as the "proletariat" versus the rest, many people would rally to the defence of their gentility, even against their true economic interest. Orwell is in fact reported by Sir Richard Rees as saying to a militant Communist who was inveighing against the *bourgeoisie*: "Look here, I'm a bourgeois and my family are bourgeois If you talk like that about them I'll punch your head."

Orwell's heaviest blows, in the *Road to Wigan Pier* and later, fall on socialist intellectuals who abandon themselves to their ideology without preserving ordinary moral scruples. He sees the violence of their opinions as the product of a position of security without responsibility.

> Though seldom giving much evidence of affection for the exploited, he [the book-trained Socialist] is perfectly capable of displaying hatred—a sort of queer, theoretical, *in vacuo* hatred—against the exploiters. Hence the grand old Socialist sport of denouncing the bourgeoisie.[3]

He further accuses the socialist intelligentsia of an obsession with power which makes them deaf to humane considerations, and indifferent to truth. The power obsession is associated with the "cult of Russia" and this, in turn, with the idea that Socialism welcomes the impersonal beehive state of the future. Orwell's own opinion was that the machine-dominated society had already arrived, and that the only choice lay between ways of organising it. There was no reason why Socialism in particular should be connected with the *Brave New World* vision which, he believed, horrified the majority of Englishmen. He argued that it should not be left to right-wing movements, themselves intent on manipulating a modern industrial society in the interests of a hierarchy, to pose as the defenders of patriotism and the traditional virtues against a left-wing materialism.

Orwell finds that the jargon of Socialism rarely connects with life as experienced by most people. He sets out to express what he believes to be true attitudes and aspirations of the working population, to make himself the spokesman for normality. He finds that Socialism can never appeal to ordinary people while it cultivates an esoteric and arrogant jargon, and while it is associated with crankishness of various sorts:

> One sometimes gets the impression that the mere words "Socialism" and "Communism" draw towards them with magnetic force every fruit-juice drinker, nudist, sandal-wearer, sex-maniac, Quaker, nature-cure quack, pacifist and feminist in England.[4]

In another context, Orwell might have cited some of these same people as part of the eccentric variety of an England he loved. Here he attacks them, because they alienate the working man by their assumption that all "progressive" attitudes go together. There may seem to be some truth in Victor Gollancz's contention that Orwell had not outgrown all the prejudices of his background, for he is making a typically "blimpish" criticism of "cranks." But, as Orwell saw, divisions of this sort are not so simple as one might think by the ease with which the labels "progressive" and "reactionary" are used; the "blimp" overlaps in his attitudes with the working-man in the public bar, who has a genuine grievance against the economic system, but sees no reason to associate with what he regards as the lunatic-fringe.

It is easy to see how *The Road to Wigan Pier* turned many people against Orwell. To the Marxist, who believed that Socialism and Communism were inevitably coming, Orwell's criticisms, if not treasonable, were at least unwise. Thus, in his Preface, Victor Gollancz refers not to the truth or untruth but to the "strange indiscretion" of Orwell's describing Russian commissars as "half-gramophones, half-gangsters." Orwell, on the other hand, did not accept the inevitability of the historical process; for him the aims of Socialism were not certain of achievement, and success depended on the power of argument to convince a sufficient number of people. From this point of view his criticisms were just and necessary.

The Socialism with which Orwell leaves us, after cutting away the accretions, is not so much a political as a moral aspiration. He believed that, whereas the intellectuals had deserted to a worship of power, the working class still based itself on moral and absolute values, which were uniting and positive forces:

> The only thing *for* which we can combine is the underlying ideal of Socialism; justice and liberty. But it is hardly strong enough to call this ideal "underlying." It is almost completely forgotten. . . . We have reached a stage when the very word "Socialism" calls up, on the one hand, a picture of aeroplanes, tractors and huge glittering factories of glass and concrete; on the other, a picture of vegetarians with wilting beards, of Bolshevik commissars (half-gramophone, half-gangster), of earnest ladies in sandals, shock-haired Marxists chewing polysyllables, escaped Quakers, birth-control fanatics and Labour Party backstairs-crawlers. Socialism, at least in this island, does not smell any longer of revolution and the overthrow of tyrants; it smells of crankishness, machine-worship and the stupid cult of Russia.[5]

Orwell brings to politics the sweeping simplicity of the moralist. He is more concerned with the impetus to change than with discussion of methods, and it is arguable that he therefore leaves the more difficult question untouched: but there can be few books on economic and social planning that read half so well as Orwell's impassioned colloquialism:

> It seemed to me then—it seems to me now, for that matter,—that economic injustice will stop the moment we want it to stop, and no sooner, and if we genuinely want it to stop the method adopted hardly matters.[6]

But although Orwell's rallying-cry of "Justice and Liberty" may be unspecific, it is not therefore meaningless. The real desire of human beings for something they call justice, regardless of the doctrine their rulers preach, responds to these words when they are shocked out of their conventional sleep by the charge of individual passion. This is what makes Orwell, though tactically he may have done some harm to the Socialist movements, one of the long-term revolutionaries, the only ones who seem to have left their mark in literature.

If Orwell was a moralist he was also a sentimentalist, though to use this word in the context of Orwell is a work of reclamation. It is used to mean that his reaction to human predicaments was emotional and immediate, and forms the criterion for his moral judgments. What it means to suffer is constantly dawning on him. Walking through a bazaar in Morocco once, he lit a cigarette and was instantly surrounded by the whole population, including the blind, clamouring for a cigarette

> In about a minute I had used up the whole packet. None of these people, I suppose, works less than twelve hours a day, and every one of them looks on a cigarette as a more or less impossible luxury.[7]

In the sense that he was not afraid of his emotions, Orwell was sentimental. In *Animal Farm*, when Boxer the carthorse sheds tears over a farm boy whom he imagines he has killed, he is reproved by Squealer, the propaganda minister, with the words "no sentimentality,

Comrade," and we are left in no doubt that this is in fact a call to stifle the natural feeling of pity.

In particular Orwell is accused of having sentimentalised the working class. In fact he insisted many times on its political incapacity and apathy: but about those aspects of the working class which he found attractive, he expressed himself with an unconcealed emotionalism which some people have found embarrassing:

> I have often been struck by the peculiar easy completeness, the perfect symmetry as it were, of a working-class interior at its best. Especially on winter evenings after tea, when the fire glows in the open range and dances mirrored in the steel fender, when Father, in shirt-sleeves, sits in the rocking-chair at one side of the fire reading the racing finals, and Mother sits on the other with her sewing, and the children are happy with a pennorth of mint humbugs, and the dog lolls roasting himself on the rag mat—it is a good place to be in, provided you can be not only in it but sufficiently *of* it to be taken for granted.[8]

It is the conservative in Orwell speaking—the man who loved Dickens and fishing, all the cosiness of the traditional England, who believed in patriotism but not jingo nationalism, in a fair deal but not in "the sacred sisters, thesis, antithesis and synthesis." In one sense of the word it may be sentiment, but it has the reality of an ideal shared by large numbers of other Englishmen who have a similar picture of how life should be lived decently.

Despite his background and education. Orwell was able to capture the tone of the common man criticising the powers-that-be over his pint, but doing it in a supremely intelligent way; he is independent, even stubborn, unwilling to be carried away by ideas, sceptical of fine phrases, but soft-hearted in his own way, a conservative by temperament, and a revolutionary only by circumstance. The more one reads of Orwell, the more one realises that he was not a root-and-branch man. He belonged, not to the minority who want to topple an entire civilisation, but to the larger number who would eradicate the chief injustices of their society but do not desire to abandon altogether the traditional moulds of their life. Where Orwell wanted change, he wanted it whole-heartedly and actively. Evolutionary and historical theories of society are not his chief concern, and people who think in these terms are inclined to see in him a heroic dead end. Political writing was for him not a branch of knowledge but a form of action in defence of standards of which he felt reasonably certain, and this certainty seems to have been rooted in an unequivocal reaction to concrete experience. Just as his conservatism is founded on love of concrete objects and ways from the past, not on abstract veneration for tradition, so it is a feeling for particular injustices, not a doctrine of progress, that makes him a revolutionary.

In each case he appealed to positives, and these gave him the firm ground from which to repudiate the dishonesties of left- and right-wing politics. If from now on his criticism of the left seems the more damaging, this may be partly due to the fact that hypocrisy is a better target for the satirist than stupidity or open self-interest. Also he came to feel more and more that the totalitarian threat in England had to be combated within the left wing. It hardly needs saying that if it is necessary to draw political lines, this is where Orwell stood. Wyndham Lewis's suggestion that in another country Orwell would have been a militant right-winger or S.S. man cannot survive the most cursory reading of any book of Orwell's, and one can only wish he had lived to reply. Orwell has been called a great critic of Socialism rather than a great socialist; considered against the background of the time in which he wrote, this description has point. He was certainly a critic, and sometimes an unfair critic, of socialists. But in a longer view he would appear as the continuer of a moral tradition to which Socialism, perhaps particularly but not exclusively in its English manifestation, has always been closely allied.

In *The Road to Wigan Pier* Orwell speaks for the first time with full confidence in his own independent standards of moral judgment applied to the political world. These were strengthened by his experiences of the Spanish Civil War, and later formed the underlying values of *Animal Farm*. If, as has been suggested. great satire supposes a better order of things, existing as an undeclared idealism alongside the order of things which is castigated, then it is belief in "Justice and Liberty" which stands behind the anger and pathos of *Animal Farm*.

REFERENCES

1. *R.W.P.*, p. 19.
2. *R.W.P.*, p. 36.
3. *R.W.P.*, p. 179.
4. *R.W.P.*, p. 173.
5. *R.W.P.*, p. 214.
6. *R.W.P.*, p. 150.
7. *E.Y.E.*, p. 145.
8. *R.W.P.*, p. 117.

CHAPTER IV

SPAIN

In *Homage to Catalonia* Orwell is at his most attractive as an autobiographical writer. It is, before all else, a record of his active physical life in Spain, and one cannot help feeling that the ebullience and optimism of the book connect directly with the stimulus of the active life. After Spain, and because of the wound received there, he was to be an onlooker, confined in the Second World War to writing articles of political comment, working for the B.B.C., and serving in the Home Guard. Many of his friends record that this was a time of frustration for him. It seems probable that the isolation from the sphere of urgent action developed his pessimism, just as in Spain the sense of human comradeship and of doing something that mattered, moved him, perhaps for the only time in his life, to a faith in men.

He had arrived in Barcelona in December 1936 with a vague idea of writing newspaper articles, but by the time members of the Left Book Club were opening their new copies of *The Road to Wigan Pier*, he had already enlisted in one of the popular militias to defend the Spanish Republic.

The atmosphere of those early days of the war in Barcelona was one to which his sympathies immediately responded: the working class seemed to be in control, the purpose of the struggle seemed clear, which, after the glutinous complexities of the English class system, must have come as a relief: "There was much that I did not understand, in some ways I did not even like it, but I recognised it immediately as a state of affairs worth fighting for."[1]

In barracks at Barcelona he was appalled at the poor equipment and training of the militias. The book has its quota of smelly latrines and lice, and the wet and the cold in the hills of Aragon: but although he describes these vividly, what dominates his memories of Spain is the experience of human contact expressed in a number of symbolic scenes. In *Homage to Catalonia*, and again in his essay "Looking Back on the Spanish Civil War," he describes his meeting with an Italian militiaman in the Lenin Barracks in Barcelona:

> I hardly know why, but I have seldom seen anyone—any man, I mean—to whom I have taken such an immediate liking. While they were talking round the table, some remark brought it out that I was a foreigner. The Italian raised his head and said quickly:
>
> "Italiano?"
>
> I answered in my bad Spanish: "No, Ingles. Y tu?"
>
> "Italiano."
>
> As we went out he stepped across the room and gripped my hand very hard. Queer, the affection you can feel for a stranger! It was as though his spirit and mine had momentarily succeeded in bridging the gulf of language and tradition and meeting in utter intimacy. I hope he liked me as well as I liked him. But I also knew that to retain my first impression of him I must not see him again; and needless to say I never did see him again. One was always making contacts of that kind in Spain.
>
> I mention this Italian militiaman because he has stuck vividly in my memory. With his shabby uniform and fierce pathetic face he typifies for me the special atmosphere of that time.[2]

Is Orwell idealising the fighting European working class, as he is accused of having idealised the English miner and the working-class home? Certainly he has none of the dreary sentiment of the official Communist tract, but one is bound to ask whether the importance he attaches to this and similar incidents of a subjective sort, does not in fact lead him to misrepresent the time he describes.

There is a special difficulty here for the critic. The atmosphere, the peculiar emotional tone of a time of revolution, is so far from the experience of the common reader and critic in Britain that acceptance or rejection of a particular writer's account becomes very much a question of temperament. The stronger tendency may be to think that since revolutions revert to a more comprehensible order of things, their spiritual atmosphere cannot be so different as is sometimes claimed. On the other hand, there is a measure of agreement in the literature of revolutions which suggests that in Orwell's account of revolutionary Barcelona there is something more than the projection of his own desire to identify himself with the working class. For example, Arturo Barea's novel *The Clash*, which deals with the same period, but in Madrid, bears out the impression of an increased emotional spontaneity in public and private life. Orwell's contention was that to live through such a time widened the emotions; he gives as an example an incident in which a ragged boy from the backstreets of Barcelona is suspected of stealing from the other members of the unit. Orwell reports the loss of some cigars, and his officer makes the boy strip and has his clothes searched. Nothing is found, and that night Orwell takes the boy to the pictures and buys him drinks, but money cannot wipe out the fact that Orwell has suspected him. Some weeks later when Orwell is a corporal and involved in a violent argument over discipline, the same boy takes his side passionately:

Why is this incident touching to me? Because in any normal circumstances it would have been impossible

> for good feelings ever to be re-established between this boy and myself. The implied accusation of theft would not have been made any better, probably somewhat worse, by my efforts to make amends. One of the effects of safe and civilized life is an immense oversensitiveness which makes all the primary emotions seem somewhat disgusting. Generosity is as painful as meanness, gratitude as hateful as ingratitude. But in Spain in 1936 we were not living in a normal time. It was a time when generous feelings and gestures were easier than they ordinarily are.[3]

Passages like this must eventually stand or fall by their truth to themselves. Orwell is always seeking out the extreme situation; the complete destitution of *Down and Out* is as remote from common experience in England as revolutionary Barcelona is. If he can convince us of the truth of what he has experienced, we are ready to tolerate greater rhetorical play with our emotions. If Orwell is one of the very few modern writers in English who can be successfully rhetorical, it must be in part because he speaks out of extreme situations, out of his own hardship and suffering. He can be lyrical without embarrassment and occasionally make a statement of faith which does not make us snigger, because we know that he is a man who can face, and has faced, the grimmest truth. When he says that it was right to encourage the Spanish Republic to fight on when the war was patently lost, or that it would be better for the British Expeditionary Force to be cut to pieces than to capitulate, words which would sound comfortable and callous from almost anyone else are not so, coming from one whose capacity for self-sacrifice we know. Inevitably the life has become an important part of the context in which we read his books.

Just as his experience of real poverty had made him

the critic of theoretic Socialism in England, so his concern with the human emotions involved in the Civil War, the desire for equality and a decent material standard of life, as he heard it expressed in the hard conditions of the Front, was to make him the bitterest enemy of the power-motive which played with these emotions as a political manoeuvre.

Orwell's experience of Spanish politics, which was what drove him to write *Homage to Catalonia*, was the result of his accidental membership of the P.O.U.M., a breakaway Marxist party on bad terms with the Communists. In the first stage of the war the Spanish Government depended for its support on a number of militias raised and directed by each party and its associated trade union. Simply because he had arrived in Barcelona with papers from the English I.L.P., Orwell found himself in the militia of the affiliated party—the P.O.U.M., and naturally enough did not consider that in the face of a common enemy it mattered in which militia you fought.

The unhappy dissensions within the Spanish Republic are complex and controversial. Orwell's explanation of things was that, as the Communists, with the prestige and strength of Russian armaments behind them, gained greater power in the Government, they suppressed social revolution so that the struggle might be presented as the simple one of Democracy versus Fascism, and thus draw the widest possible support from abroad; in other words that they sacrificed the ideals for which the working man was fighting to their own desire for power and the wish to get even with their enemies, the Anarchists.

The motives of the Spanish and foreign Communists are obscure and arguable, and as usual the strength of Orwell's case lies in his record of personal experience. What motive could possibly justify the things he saw? Returning after three and a half months to Barcelona, where his wife had come to join him, he saw street-fighting between the Republican factions, and the suppression of patently popular demonstrations in working-class areas of the city by troops sent from Valencia. The P.O.U.M. was denounced as a Fascist fifth column at a time when Orwell knew that its soldiers were fighting and being killed in the line. Later, after a further period spent at the Front, during which he was wounded, he found the P.O.U.M. proscribed, and two of his friends, a Scot and a Belgian, left to die in prison for no other reason than their chance membership of this organisation. Like other soldiers from his militia returning to Barcelona, Orwell had to sleep in the open at night for fear of showing his papers at an hotel. Finally, he and his wife, after vain intervention on behalf of their friends at the risk of their own liberty and even lives, managed to escape into France.

Spain set Orwell on his guard against the exercise of power by the left, as he had always been against power on the right. It was also the beginning of his preoccupation with the idea of objective historical truth and the fear that the very concept might be disappearing. What embittered him as much as the trumped-up accusations and secret arrests was the dishonest reporting of events in both the Spanish and English press. He saw battles reported where there had been no fighting, and troops that he had seen fighting with great bravery denounced as cowards and traitors by journalists of their own side who were following a party line. Whereas in former times the idea of objective truth had been common to people who perhaps could not agree on particular facts, it was now being jettisoned and replaced by the theory that the past was a function of present needs, and could be changed accordingly. The modern totalitarian state possessed the resources to erase all trace of a historical event, and to put a complete fabrication in its place. This thought, which is fully developed in *1984*, frightened Orwell immeasurably.

Orwell once complained that no Englishman had written a good book about totalitarianism, because to do so he would need to know it from the inside. His own time in Spain was comparatively short, and the greater part of it spent at the Front, but there is no doubt that this provided him with the inside knowledge on which he drew in *Animal Farm* and *1984*. Behind the reiterated cry of the pigs to the other animals: "Surely you don't want Jones to come back," lay Orwell's experience of a real situation in which the Spanish workers could be made to accept every encroachment on their freedom by reminding them of the supreme need to win the War.

Although one could say that most of Orwell's subsequent themes can be traced to Spain, they are not brooded on in *Homage to Catalonia*, but implicit in the action. There is no suggestion here that the tragedy is inevitable, that the working class will always be duped by its leaders. Orwell said that Spain left him with "not less but more belief in the decency of human beings." Ten years after *Homage to Catalonia*, Orwell makes Winston Smith, the hero of *1984*, write in his diary: "If there is hope, it lies in the proles," but the conclusion of that book holds out no hope at all, and Winston himself is a dupe.

Back in 1937, Orwell is closer to the action, and happier for that. Some of the most attractive passages are those which show the author himself, an earnest, methodical, very English, and therefore rather comic figure among the militiamen of Catalonia. At the beginning we see him cornering his officer in Barcelona and explaining in dreadful Spanish that he knows how to fire a rifle, but would like before going to the Front to learn how a machine-gun works. There are, of course, no machine-guns, and when the rifles are issued he is struck dumb to find himself the possessor of a German Mauser dated 1896, with a corroded barrel.

Then there is his characteristic curiosity. After reading in the foreign press that the "treacherous" P.O.U.M. has fired on the Plaza de Espana with seventy-five millimetre guns, he simply walks there and has a look; there is no sign of damage whatsoever, though none of the foreign journalists in the city seem to have taken the trouble to go and see for themselves. Most typical of all in its dedication to objectivity is his amusingly earnest account of what it is like to be shot:

> I had been about ten days at the front [this was Orwell's second stretch there] when it happened. The whole experience of being hit by a bullet is very interesting and I think it is worth describing in detail. . . . Roughly speaking it was the sensation of being *at the centre* of an explosion. There seemed to be a loud bang and a blinding flash of light all round me, and I felt a tremendous shock—no pain, only a violent shock, such as you get from an electric terminal; with it a sense of utter weakness, a feeling of being stricken and shrivelled up to nothing.[4]

After two more pages describing in detail his succession of mental states and physical sensations, he feels bound to add: "It may be, though, that if you were really dying, your thoughts would be quite different."

Alongside this dogged recorder of phenomena, there is the impulsive Orwell—a sort of Shelley masquerading as a Guards officer. This is the man who, his party proscribed and himself a fugitive, scrawls "Visca P.O.U.M." in the passageways of the smart Barcelona restaurants; just as, later, in war-time London, he was to tear down posters that demanded negotiation with Germany. This side of him comes out strongly in a passage about the street fighting in Barcelona:

> Once I had heard how things stood I felt easier in my

> mind. The issue was clear enough. On one side the C.N.T. [the Anarchist trade union] on the other the police. I have no particular love for the idealised "worker" as he appears in the bourgeois Communist's mind, but when I see an actual flesh-and-blood worker in conflict with his natural enemy, the policeman, I do have to ask myself which side I am on.[5]

This is the true fighting tone which characterises *Homage to Catalonia*. Even later, despite the loss of the war by the Republicans, and Orwell's own disillusion with many aspects of left-wing politics, Spain remains a good memory for him. In his essay of 1943 he reverts to the Italian militiaman, and in what is perhaps his best poem, comes nearest to making an affirmation of faith:

> Your name and your deeds were forgotten
> Before your bones were dry,
> And the lie that slew you is buried
> Under a deeper lie;
>
> But the thing that I saw in your face
> No power can disinherit;
> No bomb that ever bursts
> Shatters the crystal spirit.[6]

Spain seems to have brought to the surface a current of feeling which never again appears in Orwell's writing. It is a type of lyrical intensity, not elegiac as in *1984*, but suggesting, in a way that is rare in Orwell, a meaning in the events described beyond the events themselves, as if, despite the muddle and betrayal, the struggle had a purpose. On one occasion he is in a train full of wounded, being taken to a hospital far in the rear:

> We got into Tarragona as the sun was getting low. The line runs along the shore a stone's throw from the sea. As our train drew into the station, a troop-train full

of men from the International Column was drawing out, and a knot of people on the bridge were waving to them. It was a very long train, packed to bursting point with men, with field-guns lashed on the open trucks and more men clustering round the guns. I remember with peculiar vividness the spectacle of that train passing in the yellow evening light; window after window full of dark, smiling faces, the long, tilted barrels of the guns, the scarlet scarves fluttering —all this gliding slowly past us against a turquoise-coloured sea. . . .

The men who were well enough to stand had moved across the carriage to cheer the Italians as they went past. A crutch waved out of the window; bandaged forearms made the Red Salute. It was like an allegorical picture of war; the trainload of fresh men gliding proudly up the line, the maimed men sliding slowly down, and all the while the guns on the open trucks making one's heart leap as guns always do, and reviving that pernicious feeling, so difficult to get rid of, that war *is* glorious after all.[7]

REFERENCES

1. *H.T.C.*, p. 3.
2. *H.T.C.*, p. 1.
3. *E.Y.E.*, p. 160.
4. *H.T.C.*, p. 198.
5. *H.T.C.*, p. 131.
6. *E.Y.E.*, p. 176.
7. *H.T.C.*, p. 206.

CHAPTER V

THE ENGLISH REVOLUTIONARY

Orwell's next work was a reaction against the heroic position adopted in his Spanish book. It was not in any way a recantation, but the expression of a feeling that the idealistic side of human nature, if emphasised continually, led to hysteria and alienation from the way ordinary, sane people look at things:

> If you look into your own mind, which are you, Don Quixote or Sancho Panza? Almost certainly you are both. There is one part of you that wishes to be a hero or a saint, but another part of you is a little fat man who sees very clearly the advantages of staying alive with a whole skin. . . . He it is who punctures your fine attitudes and urges you to look after Number One, to be unfaithful to your wife, to bilk your debts, and so on and so forth. Whether you allow yourself to be influenced by him is a different question. But it is simply a lie to say that he is not part of you either, though most of what is said and written consists of one lie or the other, usually the first.[1]

This is taken from an essay on the "comic" coloured postcards of fat women and henpecked husbands the sort you find at the seaside, and it is to this world that the chief protagonist of Orwell's next book *Coming up for Air*, belongs. George Bowling, forty-five years old, nicknamed Tubby and Fatty, and resident in London suburbia, is an insurance agent, nagged by his wife, irritated by his children, worried endlessly about money, but resilient, not broken by the storms but still riding them, taking what he can get out of life. The first sentence of the novel sets the confidential, slightly vulgar tone: "The idea really came to me the day I got my false teeth." Although Tubby Bowling's chief preoccupations are keeping out of trouble, affording the odd extra drink, and trying to conceal from his wife the occasional infidelity, he is naturally shrewd, free from illusions about himself, and critical of the society around him. In fact he is the intelligent ordinary man envisaged in *The Road to Wigan Pier*; he knows and cares little about socialist theory, is antagonised by such left-wingers as he meets, but nevertheless stands to gain by a reorganisation of society and is acute enough to see this. But he is by no stretch of the imagination a revolutionary; he goes through life sceptically aware of the political and economic swindles practised on him, but accepts these, for all practical purposes, as permanent features of a not very congenial world. He knows instinctively that war is coming and can imagine vividly what it will be like when it comes, but he has no opinions about policy, if only because he is too busy making a living and paying his bills. Like earlier Orwell heroes, George Bowling is against the society he lives in, but unlike them he is only passively against it. He is still very much an Orwellian hero, but older, more sceptical and with a sense of humour about himself.

The redressing of the balance in Orwell's mind in favour of passivity seems to have coincided with an interest in Henry Miller, whom he had met in Paris on his way to Spain in 1936. Orwell records that he was intrigued to find someone who felt no interest at all in the Spanish war. He told Orwell that his ideas about combating Fascism, defending democracy and so on, were baloney, since our civilisation was going to be swept away and replaced by some barely human way of life. Orwell never took this attitude as a man; he always believed that it was worth putting up a fight, but his experience in Spain made him wonder whether

Miller was not, after all, right, and that the positio
of the writer, *qua* writer, must be one of passivity. I
Inside the Whale Orwell defends the argument that th
writer's task is to accept, record, endure, but not preten
to control the world process: to recognise that one i
inside the Leviathan of modern history, being carrie
in a direction one does not approve. Any novel, say
Orwell, that attempts to be more positive, is likely t
be emotionally spurious.

Coming Up for Air is an attempt at the novel of passivity
Although Orwell's social preoccupations inevitabl
appear, they are in the form of negative criticism no
constructive suggestion. The bare structure of the stor
is quickly described. With seventeen pounds (won o
a horse) tucked away unknown to his wife, Georg
Bowling casts about for a pleasant way to spend it
Various accidents recall his boyhood in the Oxfordshir
village of Lower Binfield, and, deciding to spend th
money on a visit there, he eventually sets out. Befor
he does so, however, a flashback occupying half th
book describes his childhood and adolescence in th
village as he remembers them, and, more briefly, hi
service in the First World War, his subsequent hun
for a job, and marriage.

Telling his wife that he has been called to Birminghan
on business, he drives off one day only to find that th
village has become a raw new town where each succes
sive detail shatters his nostalgia. He returns home t
the routine life and routine row with his wife, who has
as usual, detected his trickery and suspects the worst
"Nothing remained except a vulgar low-down row in a
smell of old mackintoshes."

It is an uneven book. The incidents in his visit t
Lower Binfield make their point in a rather tiresome an
repetitive way and are far less effective than the evoca
tion of moods in his childhood, where Orwell is no
obliged to tell a consecutive story. For the villag

background he must have drawn extensively on his own experience of village storekeeping in Essex; George Bowling is made to be the son of a shopkeeper. Yet some of the finest pieces of evocation cannot have come from his own experience. Here George Bowling is remembering his parents:

> I can see them now. A Sunday afternoon—summer, of course, always summer—a smell of roast pork and greens still floating in the air, and Mother on one side of the fireplace, starting off to read the latest murder but gradually falling asleep with her mouth open, and Father on the other, in slippers and spectacles, working his way slowly through yards of smudgy print. And the soft feeling of summer all round you, the geranium in the window, a starling somewhere, and myself under the table with the *B.O.P.*, making believe that the tablecloth is a tent.[2]

And then there are many good passages about fishing:

> Christ, those fishing days! The hot sticky afternoons in the big schoolroom when I've sprawled across my desk, with old Blowers's voice grating away about predicates and subjunctives and relative clauses, and all that's in my mind is the backwater near Burford Weir and the green pool under the willows with the dace gliding to and fro. And then the terrific rush on bicycles after tea, up Chamford Hill and down to the river to get in an hour's fishing before dark. The still summer evening, the faint splash of the weir, the rings on the water where the fish are rising, the midges eating you alive, the shoals of dace swarming round your hook and never biting. And the kind of passion with which you'd watch the black backs of the fish swarming round, hoping, praying (yes, literally praying) that one of them would change his mind and grab your bait before it got too dark.[3]

Passages like these are undoubtedly convincing in thei main purpose, which is to express the intense nostalgi of one particular middle-aged man, but Orwell canno entirely avoid more general social considerations. It i not mere nostalgia; the world really *has* changed a George Bowling has grown older. The country has bee built up, small businesses like his father's have bee bought out by chain stores, fishing has become eithe a crowded affair on the banks of canals, or else a ric man's privilege. Did Lower Binfield with its bad sanita tion and flies not perhaps have some real advantag over his suburban semi-detached? In a chrome an plastic milk-bar George Bowling bites into a frankfurte and finds that it is filled with fish; he realises that thi is where industrial progress has brought us—to celluloi and chrome-plate, everything streamlined and slick an false.

Together with the change in the physical details o life, George Bowling (and Orwell) felt that a whol climate of cosiness and security and continuity wa disappearing. The mental world of George Bowling' parents rested on solid, if unexpressed, values lik ordinary decency. Trade might be bad, life might b hard, but they preserved to the verge of bankruptcy th conviction that effort brought reward, that howeve unfortunate some individuals might be, the genera order of life they had known would be preserved. I is a moral order, not conceived in terms of principle bu institutionalised in traditional ways and assumptions that Orwell records and laments, and he finds it in separable from its English accidentals, from stewed tea Yorkshire pudding, and apple dumplings.

Orwell was not the man to ignore the unpleasan things in the past. He knew that the life of Edwardia villages rested on penniless farmworkers and, mor remotely, on tubercular miners and starving coolies There is nothing, even in his most nostalgic writing, tha suggests he for a moment considered these things as mere blemishes on an attractive rural picture. But he hoped that something might be preserved to humanise the new machine civilisation. The whole of *Coming up for Air*, and passages scattered throughout the essays—on "Boys Weeklies," "Raffles and Miss Blandish," "Dickens," "The art of Donald McGill," "The Decline of the English Murder," and also the splendid last paragraph of *Homage to Catalonia*—all reveal a strong affection for the details of traditional English life; and he includes not only the country but the old industrial towns with their corner pubs and small, dusty shops and the acres of allotments, all the ramshackle variety which he believed was somehow bound up with the gentleness of the English and their respect for law. In the June 1940 number of *The Adelphi* he reviewed Jack Hilton's *English Ways*, and what he said there can stand for what he expressed on many occasions:

> But chiefly it is valuable for its glimpses of English working-class life in the late capitalist age, of the England of totes, dog-races, football-pools, Woolworths, the pictures, Gracie Fields, Walls ice cream, potato crisps, celanese stockings, dart-boards, pin-tables, cigarettes, cups of tea, and Saturday evenings in the four-ale bar. Lord knows how much of this civilisation, founded upon foreign investments and neglected agriculture, can survive, but it was a good civilisation while it lasted, and the people who grew up in it will carry some of their gentleness and decency into the iron ages that are coming.[4]

If Orwell seems to concentrate on working-class life it is because he sees the working class as conserving most tenaciously what he considers the English virtues. They are the last repository of that indeterminate but solid virtue, decency, in an age when power-worship and the cult of violence are invading society. He sees the working man's sense of common decency as the obverse of his political passivity. He cannot think in terms of power and party, and therefore he cannot hate. Chesterton, whom Orwell had certainly read, put it this way: "the poor are always at the tail of the procession, and whether they are morally worse or better depends on whether humanity as a whole is proceeding towards heaven or hell."[5] Orwell had little doubt where the chief ideological movements of his time were leading.

It is the intellectuals who hate. George Bowling accompanies his wife to a Left Book Club meeting to hear "Mr So-and-So, the well-known anti-Fascist." His description of the speaker shooting propaganda at him like a human barrel-organ, and always with a message of hate, is a clear foretaste of the "two-minutes hate" which is one of the institutions of *1984*.

Immediately after the Left Book Club meeting George Bowling visits his friend Porteous, a retired public-school master. Porteous's remoteness from modern life might perhaps be credible in a main character developed throughout the book, but in the few pages where we meet him he never comes to life and has clearly been drawn in to illustrate a point. This seems to be that the cultivated English gentleman, fixated on the "eternal verities" and on the past, is himself a ghost from the past, unable to conceive that things are about to change out of all recognition, and that a ruthless, streamlined totalitarianism is coming to erase the civilisation he knows. "Dead men and live gorillas," thinks George Bowling, "there doesn't seem to be anything in between."

There the problem rests. Perhaps we are to think that the best hope for the future lies in people like George Bowling himself, who carry in them a feeling for what is alive and valuable in the English tradition, and have therefore a natural resistance to the gorillas and streamlined men. But part of this strength is his passivity, and Orwell, wisely, does not force on his character any hint of offering a solution: "What's the future got to do with you and me? Holding down our jobs—that's our future."[6]

Coming up for Air proved Orwell's most popular book so far; and deservedly, for it is a much maturer book than his earlier novels about England. Unlike these it has humour and tolerance for people, and, in Tubby Bowling, a central figure who, apart from voicing many of the author's sentiments, sticks in the mind in his own right. This is not to suggest that by the highest standards of character-creation he is anything more than cardboard. John Wain fixes Orwell's peculiar excellence in this direction when he suggests that *Coming Up for Air*, like *Animal Farm*, exemplifies Orwell's "genuine flair for making the emblem live in its own right without ceasing to be emblematic."[7]

In the same essay John Wain insists on the centrality of this novel to all Orwell's work. If we are to consider the ideas statically, this can hardly be denied; sympathy for the ordinary life and the simple pleasures, criticism of the social system, fear of the future, and above all, as Wain's essay brings out admirably, nostalgia for pastoral England, are all there. What is missing, however, is the dynamic Orwell, the political activist, who with all his nostalgia still believed that there were moments when you must choose and act.

Such a moment seemed to have come in 1940. Within a few months of the publication of his novel war was declared, and the new situation with its sharpening of national consciousness encouraged Orwell to think that the time had come for a positive reorientation of British society amounting to a revolution. The time for action had come, and the form of writing he now chose was the pamphlet.

The Lion and the Unicorn (1940), now at last republished in its entirety, has to be taken as the dynamic complement to *Coming up for Air*. Of its three sections—"England your England," "Shopkeepers at War," and "The English Revolution,"—the second two are polemical and have largely been proved wrong by events, while the first, which is introductory and descriptive, is immediately recognisable as one of the classic essays on England, and has been collected separately among his essays. Almost any passage illustrates not only his powers of observation and his comprehensiveness, but his love for England:

> The clatter of clogs in the Lancashire mill towns, the to-and-fro of the lorries on the Great North Road, the queues outside the Labour Exchanges, the rattle of pin-tables in the Soho pubs, the old maids biking to Holy Communion through the mists of the autumn mornings—all these are fragments, but *characteristic* fragments of the English scene.[8]

This is recognisably the author of *Coming up for Air*. Particularly in those few extra words lavished on the old maids, you see Orwell's affection for the old-fashioned in England. But now he has a dynamic purpose, and is careful to distinguish the established and conventionally traditional from what he considers really vital and permanent in England. He finds a comparison which expresses the need for change, but rules out complete disruption: "A family with the wrong members in control—that, perhaps, is as near as one can come to describing England in a phrase." This idea of the family appears again in an amusing but penetrating remark about two sub-sections of the middle-class, the "Blimps" and the left-wing intelligentsia. Though symbolically opposite types, they are he says, linked: "in any case they are born to a considerable extent into the same families."[9]

Similarly, in the paragraph quoted next, the image of the "everlasting animal" apart from providing the conceptual parallel, carries, because it is something living, the warmth of the author's feeling:

> The Stock Exchange will be pulled down, the horse plough will give way to the tractor, the country houses will be turned into children's holiday camps, the Eton and Harrow match will be forgotten, but England will still be England, an everlasting animal stretching into the future and the past, and, like all living things, having the power to change out of all recognition and yet remain the same.[10]

In the next two sections Orwell considered how England could transform itself. He believed the War provided the conditions for a socialist revolution, indeed that the War could not be won with the old capitalist structure and leadership. Going further, he suggested that, rather than accept the radical social and economic changes necessary for winning the War, the English upper classes would make a compromise agreement with Germany.

To-day this sounds extreme and far-fetched. There is no defending Orwell against the charge of being wrong. But why was he wrong? Was he entirely out of touch with the England which was his theme? The answer must be, partly, that in choosing to write about political developments in time of war, when there was little political or military information available, he was committing himself to surmise and the assessment of probabilities. A further explanation of the lack of proportion in parts of *The Lion and the Unicorn*, and in articles for the American left-wing *Partisan Review*, may be found in the discontent of his own life at the time. Rejected on medical grounds by all three Services, he had to content himself with the Home Guard, of which it is said he was an earnest member. Later in the War he broadcast to India for the B.B.C., but at first he had to continue a life of book-reviewing and article-writing at a time when he believed he should be doing something urgent and useful. The overstrained tone of some of the writing may therefore indicate that it was a substitute for action.

Having said this, it is worth adding that his prophecies, though wrong, were not necessarily absurd. In fact they were never put to the test. He wrote while it still seemed possible that Russia would collapse before the first German advance, and before the American declaration of war. Orwell imagined invasion, an attempt at a negotiated peace by the right-wing and, in the face of this, a working-class revolution, inspired by motives partly social, partly patriotic. No one can say what might have been the extent of collaboration after an invasion, nor from what section of the community the real resistance would have come.

Orwell did not deny that a socialist England too might be defeated, but he thought it would be harder to defeat because people would be fighting for themselves:

"It will fight in such a way that even if it is beaten its memory will be dangerous to the victor, as the memory of the French Revolution was dangerous to Metternich's Europe."[11]

In *The Lion and the Unicorn* Orwell was more specific than he had before been in describing the changes he wanted. They included such things as nationalisation of the major industries and of land over 15 acres, the limitation of incomes so that the highest did not exceed the lowest by more than ten to one, democratic reform of the educational system, and various liberal proposals concerning the colonies. But he does not involve himself in great detail, and insists, typically, that, though necessary, these things are nothing in themselves, and that the nation must grow together, recognise the injustice in its own midst, realise its own power to change things so as to remove these injustices. He places his chief hope on the equality of sacrifice which war brings.

Some of Orwell's statements are still controversial, but how long will they be so? Who can now get angry about, or even understand, the issues in Swift's *Conduct of the Allies*? If we are not going to reduce the greatness of a pamphlet to a question of rhetorical syntax we must look for some elusive quality of intensity or elevation of feeling which leaves its mark on the form even when the subject-matter is dead. The great discovery that inspires Orwell in this pamphlet is that it is again possible to be patriotic. In a war against Fascism, Socialism and patriotism have become the same thing. Love for England, for all the items of his affectionate catalogues, can now combine with the desire of the George Bowlings of England for a fair and decent society:

> Patriotism has nothing to do with Conservatism. It is actually the opposite of Conservatism, since it is devotion to something that is always changing and yet is felt to be mystically the same.[12]

The pamphlet is a kind of fulfilment, however brief and unstable. Two streams which Orwell had been constantly trying to reconcile come together—the traditional, nostalgic, patriotic stream which connects with his hold on concrete objects and the descriptiveness of his style; and the revolutionary, the visionary stream, which is what gives his writing passionate movement and force. The feeling that England was approaching a moment of great change fused the two. There is a Miltonic *élan* in the radicalism of the closing paragraph, but alongside it one can sense Orwell's firm foundation in England. Perhaps he would not have been altogether ashamed of the adjective "Churchillian":

> The heirs of Nelson and Cromwell are not in the House of Lords. They are in the fields and streets, in the factories and the armed forces, in the four-ale bar and

the suburban back-garden; and at present they are still kept under by a generation of ghosts. Compared with the task of bringing the real England to the surface even the winning of the war, necessary though it is, is secondary. There is no question of stopping short, salvaging 'democracy' standing still. Nothing ever stands still. We must add to our heritage or lose it, we must grow greater or grow less, we must go forward or go backward. I believe in England, and I believe we shall go forward.[13]

REFERENCES

1. *C.E.*, p. 108.
2. *C.U.A.*, p. 47.
3. *C.U.A.*, p. 73.
4. *The Adelphi*, Jun. 1940.
5. G. K. Chesterton, *The Victorian Age in Literature*, 1946 reset impression, p. 51.
6. *C.U.A.*, p. 229.
7. John Wain, *Essays on Literature and Ideas*, 1963, p. 206.
8. *L.A.U.*, p. 10.
9. *L.A.U.*, p. 35.
10. *L.A.U.*, p. 44.
11. *L.A.U.*, p. 87.
12. *L.A.U.*, p. 87.
13. *L.A.U.*, p. 96.

CHAPTER VI

POLITICS AND LITERATURE

Orwell wrote only two more books, the ones on which his reputation chiefly rests—*Animal Farm* and *1984*. Each continues the line of his earlier political and social preoccupations, and can quite legitimately be analysed in terms of these. But quite as important as the expressed ideas are the assumptions about political writing which underlie these, his most influential, works. Fortunately Orwell made these assumptions explicit in a number of articles about the relationship of the writer to politics; and only slightly less explicit in his own literary criticism. It is these two groups of essays which we must now consider.

The first group is very largely the sustained juxtaposition of two convictions which Orwell held with equal strength. One is what we should expect from the pamphleteer and man of action:

> My starting-point is always a feeling of partisanship, a sense of injustice. When I sit down to write a book, I do not say to myself, "I am going to produce a work of art." I write it because there is some lie I want to expose, some fact to which I want to draw attention, and my initial concern is to get a hearing.[1]

There was bound, at times, to be difficulty in reconciling this urgent purpose with the more aesthetic considerations of which Orwell was well aware. But this was not the real conflict. He had made up his mind to sacrifice literary polish and unity of form where this was necessary. He admitted that the long sections of *Homage to Catalonia* that go into the intricacies of Spanish politics and quote newspaper-cuttings in the attempt to defend the P.O.U.M., would lose their interest for the ordinary reader after a few years. But he could not omit these sections, for they were the reason for writing the book:

> "I happened to know, what very few people in England had been allowed to know, that innocent men were being falsely accused. If I had not been angry about that I should never have written the book."[2]

But if he was prepared to sacrifice literary accomplishment to politics, he was not prepared to sacrifice the individual integrity which was for him the essence of a writer. This was the conviction which he had to reconcile with his political activism:

> No tirades against "individualism" and the "ivory tower", no pious platitudes to the effect that "true individualism is only attainable through identification with the community" can get over the fact that a bought mind is a spoiled mind.[3]

Orwell looked at literature as a tradition of great independents, and this separated him from those writers of the nineteen-thirties who wanted to submerge their individuality in the social struggle, although he shared many of their specific preoccupations. Orwell's background, his early isolation in Burma, his rather conservative reading list when a young man (so far as we can tell)—Wells, Gissing, Kipling, Dickens, and the eighteenth-century novelists—all this kept him outside politics until his root attitudes were already formed. He was thirty-three before he wrote his first explicitly political book, *The Road to Wigan Pier*, but he had the ambition to be a writer long before he felt the urgency of putting the social order right. Indeed it comes as a shock to find how purely literary was his early published work in *The Adelphi*: literary allusion and contrived similes drop heavily from his pen, and in an issue otherwise devoted to socialist topics he writes a study of Lord Byron. On this early evidence one might have predicted for him a small place among the less exciting and traditional authors of his generation; indeed, technically, he was never very experimental. But political awareness was forced upon him by his own experience of poverty, so that he came to believe political action a duty. His difficulty was that he entered political argument at a time when parties and movements were massing against each other, and had no place in their ideologies for an independent. Concern with individual integrity was considered dangerous self-indulgence, but for Orwell it was certainly not this, for it had to co-exist in painful tension with his other deeply-held conviction that the writer must take part in political life.

Orwell's resolution of the tension was in fact no resolution at all; it consisted in establishing two standards, rather as a Christian might—one for making choices between courses of political action, choices which by the very nature of politics were between degrees of evil; the other, a more Olympian standard, which placed the world *sub specie aeternitatis* and judged by an absolute standard of truth, regardless of immediate advantage. The writer, according to Orwell, had a duty to consider both standards. Like any other man he should be prepared to take part in the corrupting business of politics, since it is clearly preferable that certain courses of action should be chosen rather than others: but *as writer* he must reserve the right to stand back and tell the whole truth. Because of this reservation the political writer would always be "an individual, an outsider, at the most an unwelcome guerrilla on the flank of a regular army." Orwell's own practice conformed so well with this formula at times that, in true guerrilla fashion, he was a greater embarrassment to his friends than to his enemies.

It would be a pity to use Orwell's literary criticism merely to further discussion of his views on political writing, since his writings on Swift, Dickens, and Kipling are perhaps the best single essays on their subjects: best, not in the sense that they are the most comprehensive or the most fair, but that, like Dr Johnson's or G. K. Chesterton's, they register the total response of a mature personality in robust and memorable terms. The last paragraph of his essay on Dickens sticks in the mind particularly as one of those places where the veils of literary criticism are torn aside and the writer achieves a direct and personal confrontation with his subject.

Once we analyse Orwell's critical method, we are back to the double standard. He makes a socio-political judgment on an author, and then a literary judgment, and his essays consist of a dialogue between these two points of view. Thus Yeats, Eliot, and Kipling are all condemned as reactionaries by one standard, but at the same time he recognises that they are authors with a power to make him respond.

His normal approach to an author is in terms of his message. For him, all art takes up a political position, not least that of the "Art for Art's sake" school. Writing about Dickens, for example, the chief questions he asks are these: how far was Dickens a serious critic of nineteenth-century institutions, how far someone who looked in the first place for a change of heart? He concludes that Dickens's attitudes to change were largely conditioned by his *petit bourgeois* outlook. Summarised thus, his method seems to be that of the dreariest Marxist criticism, but in practice he works up to his general statements from detailed observations about the writing and is never dogmatic. Here are some typical remarks of Orwell's:

> It is not merely a coincidence that Dickens never writes about agriculture and writes endlessly about food. He was a Cockney, and London is the centre of the earth in rather the same sense that the belly is the centre of the body. It is a city of consumers, of people who are deeply civilized but not primarily useful.[4]

> When Dickens has once described something you see it for the rest of your life. But in a way the concreteness of his vision was a sign of what he is missing. For, after all, that is what the merely casual onlooker always sees—the outward appearance, the non-functional, the surface of things. No-one who is really involved in the landscape ever sees the landscape. Wonderfully as he describes an *appearance*, Dickens does not often describe a *process*. The vivid pictures that he succeeds in leaving in one's memory are nearly always the pictures of things seen in leisure moments, in the coffee-rooms of country inns or through the windows of a stage-coach; the kind of thing he notices are inn-signs, brass door-knockers, painted jugs, the interiors of shops and private houses, clothes, faces and, above all, food.
>
> Everything is seen from the consumer-angle.[5]

The strength of this approach is that it connects with life outside the conventional terms of literary criticism; and at the same time Orwell manages to avoid making literature merely illustrative of social history, precisely because he has developed this capacity to keep his literary judgments from being drawn in the wake of his political convictions. However radical his disagreement with the implications of Yeats's or Eliot's poetry, he can still maintain his enthusiasm for "The Second

Coming" or the last lines of "The Love Song of J. Alfred Prufrock," because he does not pretend that something undesirable in tendency is therefore unattractive as literature. For this reason he can be extremely generous to writers whose arguments he has attacked fiercely. Thus after accusing H. G. Wells of a complete inability to understand the modern world—"since 1920 he has squandered his talents in slaying paper dragons" —he adds: "But how much it is, after all, to have any talents to squander." The mature type of literary judgment which Orwell evolved, recognising the criterion of a writer's sincerity and intensity of vision, but reserving the right to call him wrong, or at least half right, meant that he could be lively, polemical, and convinced, but without bullying his reader or distorting the facts.

His most explicit writing on the subject comes in his essay on Swift:

> From what I have written it may have seemed that I am *against* Swift, and that my object is to refute him and belittle him. In a political and moral sense I am against him, so far as I understand him. Yet curiously enough he is one of the writers I admire with least reserve, and *Gulliver's Travels*, in particular, is a book which it seems impossible for me to grow tired of.[6]

> The explanation must be that Swift's world-view is felt to be *not* altogether false—or it would probably be more accurate to say, not false all the time. Swift is a diseased writer. He remains permanently in a depressed mood, rather as if someone suffering from jaundice or the after-effects of influenza should have the energy to write books. But we all know that mood, and something in us responds to the expression of it.[7]

> The durability of *Gulliver's Travels* goes to show that,

> if the force of belief is behind it, a world-view that only just passes the test of sanity is sufficient to produce a great work of art.[8]

:t followed from Orwell's double standard of judgment hat he saw his own political writing as an attempt to ind an honourable solution to the conflicting claims of olitical urgency and literary truth, but he never lescribed in detail how he set about achieving this. Ie did say, however, of *Animal Farm* that it was the irst book in which he tried, with full consciousness of vhat he was doing, to fuse political purpose and artistic urpose, and since the general verdict has been that in his book he succeeded perfectly, it is worth looking losely at how this was achieved.

The political impulse behind *Animal Farm* was to xplode the Soviet myth. Spain had disillusioned Orwell .bout the motives of Communists, and shown him nough of their methods to make him understand what vas really happening in the Russian purges. The Nazi-oviet Pact served to confirm him in his belief that there vas only one enemy, totalitarianism; and when, later, ussia was invaded and became Britain's ally, Orwell vas unenthusiastic. So unpopular was the position he ook up that, when he completed *Animal Farm* in 'ebruary 1944, he could find no publisher. Its publiation a year later coincided with the beginning of eneral disillusionment in the West with the Soviet Jnion, and the swing of opinion soon turned it into a est-seller, translated into several languages, and ringing Orwell the first appreciable sums of money e ever received from writing.

The story is too well-known for anything but a brief ımmary to be given here. A farmer is driven out by is animals, who undertake the organisation of the farm or the benefit of all. But, inevitably, government falls nder the control of the pigs, the most intelligent but at

the same time the most unscrupulous of the animal
By a combination of hypocrisy and ruthlessness the
establish a tyranny, at least the equal of the one they hav
replaced, and themselves enjoy all the privileges of th
hated humans. At the end of the book, the pigs, who b
now walk on their hind legs, are entertaining th
neighbouring human tyrants. The other animals loo
pathetically in through the farmhouse window: "Th
creatures outside looked from pig to man, from man t
pig, and from pig to man again; but already it wa
impossible to say which was which."

Trotsky and Stalin, the purges, and the sudde
reversals of policy are all there, unmistakably, and ye
Animal Farm is quite clearly not a political book in th
same sense as *Homage to Catalonia* and *The Road to Wiga
Pier* are. The form is, of course, decisive; it is not merel
another, indirect, way of conveying the same politica
message, but alters the thing said. Orwell sub-titled th
book "A Fairy Story," but if we call it what it really is
an animal fable, it immediately appears in its prope
tradition—like the majority of animal fables it is a mora
tale. The political impulse is, as it were, outside the boo
itself; it lies in the choice of the subject-matter and i
the decision to write at all. Once these decisions hav
been made, Orwell can concentrate on observing th
convention.

Animals have one great advantage for the moralist—
they can easily be equated with single qualities: the fo
with cunning, the lion with strength; in other words the
present a convenient simplification of the human world
convenient because a moral vision *is* a simplification o
the complex happenings of life (though perhaps a
illuminating one). The animal fable suits Orwell so wel
because he is able to write by his higher standard o
pure moral integrity. It is the moral decisions in politica
life that he is always concerned with, and here he ha
found a form which permits him to ignore everythin

else. *Animal Farm* does not allow for the necessities which must always in some measure force the hand of even the most despotic rulers; these lie outside its convention, which is moral. Had Orwell chosen a more discursive form he would have felt bound to consider every objection of this sort, if only afterwards to discount it.

The observance of the convention in *Animal Farm* is a skilful act of balance. The animals must be close enough to their human patterns for easy recognition, yet not so close as to invite complex speculations about motive and the psychological depths of their personalities, which are outside the scope of the convention. The emphasis must vary so that the reader is only asked to interpret at certain points. Some details are clearly there for themselves alone, as when we are told that Mr Jones sits on a *Windsor* chair, or that Napoleon is a *Berkshire* boar; the concrete detail and the circumstantial irrelevance are the basis of the atmosphere of authenticity which must be built up before the story can hold any of the weight of allegorical meaning.

On the allegorical plane it certainly helps to have some acquaintance with Russian history since the October Revolution. Even though the moral pattern of events in the book stands by itself, and will no doubt do so when the historical models have passed out of common knowledge, there is undeniable pleasure to be gained from going a little further than the most obvious correlations, Napoleon/Stalin and Snowball/Trotsky, and discovering the New Economic Plan and the controversy over agricultural and industrial priorities. But more important than a detailed knowledge of Russian history is some familiarity with the language and methods of Marxist argument, without which one loses the full flavour of passages such as the following:

> After much thought Snowball declared that the Seven Commandments could in effect be reduced to a single

> maxim, namely: "Four legs good, two legs bad." This, he said, contained the essential principle of Animalism. Whoever had thoroughly grasped it would be safe from human influences. The birds at first objected, since it seemed to them that they also had two legs, but Snowball proved to them that this was not so.
>
> "A bird's wing, comrades," he said, "is an organ of propulsion and not of manipulation. It should therefore be regarded as a leg. The distinguished mark of Man is the *hand*, the instrument with which he does all his mischief."[9]

Just as basic to the convention as the assumption that animals are simple moral figures, good or bad, is the assumption that they are funny. Indeed the two things are connected because the transparency of their motives, compared with the web of human self-justification, is comic while at the same time forming part of the essential moral clarification of the world. Of course the animals are not funny all the time—they can also be pathetic and beautiful—but only when we remember that they are acting in a human way. In short passages scattered throughout *Animal Farm* Orwell keeps up the light-hearted tone necessary for the convention. Some of these have the extra merit of giving us a laugh at the expense of the pigs, as when Squealer, the propaganda minister, falls off the ladder while altering the Commandments: but at other times even the noblest characters are ridiculed: we are told, for instance, that Boxer, the devoted, hard-working cart-horse, has difficulty in learning the alphabet: by the time he had learnt E, F, G, H, he had forgotten A, B, C, and D.

The ridiculing of the animals is utterly necessary, for only by taking them as a joke can we possibly take them seriously. If asked to read a serious account of their activities, we should certainly at some point find them ridiculous. The author's art lies in himself deciding when we shall laugh, in timing the laughs so that in the intervals the serious passages can have their effect. Sometimes the alternation can be surprisingly sudden, and effective by contrast, as during the confessions and purges on the farm:

> Then a sheep confessed to having urinated in a drinking pool—urged to do this, so she said, by Snowball—and two other sheep confessed to having murdered an old ram, an especially devoted follower of Napoleon, by chasing him round and round a bonfire when he was suffering from a cough. They were all slain on the spot. And so the tale of confessions and executions went on, until there was a pile of corpses lying before Napoleon's feet and the air was heavy with the smell of blood, which had been unknown there since the expulsion of Jones.[10]

To recognise the convention in which *Animal Farm* is written is to make irrelevant certain sorts of critical remark. Thus Richard Rees writes of Orwell that "by comparing the working-class to animals, even noble and attractive ones, he implies that they are at an irremediable disadvantage in the class struggle." But in choosing a convention you choose to obey its rules, and by the rules of the animal fable animals are inevitably pathetic at least some of the time. It is quite another thing to say, however, that having chosen the form, Orwell took full advantage of the opportunities for pathos. Besides being representative of simple qualities, animals inspire simple emotions of affection and pity; it seems true, if curious, that it is often possible to feel more frankly emotional about animals than about human beings. No one has accused Orwell of sentimentality in *Animal Farm*, as they have in the case of the Italian militiaman of *Homage to Catalonia*, or the miners of *The Road to Wigan Pier*. It is a part of the atmosphere of the book that just as qualities are simple and well-defined, so feelings too are simple, deep, and uninhibited. When Boxer, the loyal cart-horse who has carried the main burden of the farm's work, is sold by the pigs to the knacker, we weep for the terrible pity of it like children who meet injustice for the first time.

There is another way in which the animal allegory suits Orwell—it provides him with a pastoral setting. The question of Revolution is nicely separated from industrialism, which was something Orwell was not fond of, quite apart from its capitalist manifestation. In *Animal Farm*, industry is neatly symbolised by the windmill, which, however, in no way transforms the landscape. The aim of the Revolution, as expressed in its song, was the creation of a pastoral paradise:

> Bright will shine the fields of England,
> Purer will its waters be . . .

reminiscent of that forgotten clause of the Communist Manifesto which promises the eradication of the difference between town and country. And as the book progresses, the descriptions of the beauty of the fields present an ever more pathetic contrast to the terror and slaughter of the pigs' regime.

Alone of Orwell's books *Animal Farm* is free of his own dramatised personality. Elsewhere he is either present himself or else closely identified with the hero, and in some particular stance: as Gordon Comstock, the defiant failure, or George Bowling, the personification of shrewd common sense, or in his own role of convinced revolutionary in *Homage to Catalonia*. These *personae* were part of Orwell's style, giving it energy and individuality, but they were also a flaw in the formal unity of his books; for each stance represented only one aspect of Orwell's thinking, and his honesty always made him include the criticism of that stance, so that every book, apart from *Animal Farm*, contains its own contradictions. This is why, choosing one's passages, one can present Orwell as a revolutionary or a conservative, an idealist or a sceptic.

Animal Farm is unique among his books for its unity, its formal perfection. This is no doubt partly due to the power of the convention to exclude some of Orwell's preoccupations, but even more to its power to absorb and hold in suspension so many of his diverse qualities. In *Animal Farm* we find, not in conflict but in proportion, as they are needed for the preservation of the convention, Orwell's humour and his pessimism, his tenderness and his anger, his idealism and his scepticism. It is even possible to discover a truly "Orwellian" figure, here not a *persona* of the author, but distanced and reduced to the status of a minor character, included as some painters have included themselves in the corner of a large canvas. This is Benjamin the donkey, with his warm heart and his sceptical motto: "Donkeys live a long time."

REFERENCES

1. *E.Y.E.*, p. 13.
2. *E.Y.E.*, p. 14.
3. *E.Y.E.*, p. 132.
4. *C.E.*, p. 35.
5. *C.E.*, p. 38.
6. *S.A.E.*, p. 78.
7. *S.A.E.*, p. 81.
8. *S.A.E.*, p. 83.
9. *A.F.*, p. 27.
10. *A.F.*, p. 28.

CHAPTER VII

THE ORWELLIAN TENSION

It seems right, before sinking into the nightmare world of Orwell's last book *1984*, to record the happier side of his character as it appears in the reminiscences of his friends. None of those who have written about him give the impression of having known him intimately, and their anecdotes are not of the sort that yield deep perceptions into a man's character: but almost without exception they endear him to the reader, recording as they do his thoughtfulness and kindness, his capacity for enjoying unsophisticated pleasures, and sometimes his obstinate determination to look on the black side of things. T. R. Fyvel, who succeeded Orwell as literary editor of *Tribune*,[1] recalls that he found a drawer full of unsuitable but well-intentioned contributions which Orwell had not had the heart to reject, while Paul Potts remembers during the same period seeing him on two occasions slip money of his own into the envelopes he was returning. It is also Paul Potts who in his autobiography gives this wonderful description of Orwell at high-tea in winter, in his living-room in Canonbury Square:

> A huge fire, the table crowded with marvellous things, Gentleman's Relish and various jams, kippers, crumpets and toast. And always the Gentleman's Relish, with its peculiar unique flat jar and the Latin inscription on the label. Next to it stood the Coopers-Oxford marmalade pot. He thought in terms of vintage tea and had the same attitude to bubble and squeak as a Frenchman has to Camembert . . . There was

> something very innocent and terribly simple about him.[2]

Orwell would have been pleased with this account. He liked to think of himself as basically genial but forced by the circumstances of the time into bitter political controversy. He once wrote a poem beginning:

> A happy vicar I might have been
> Two hundred years ago,
> To preach upon eternal doom
> And watch my walnuts grow.[3]

John Raymond dismisses this as Orwell's favourite pleasant delusion and sees him rather as in the Scots Nonconformist tradition, a dreadful elder of the Kirk.[4] Evidence could be found in Orwell's writings to support this view, but the selection would be one-sided. Orwell was in fact both the happy vicar and the Kirk elder, which is to say that he was neither of the true types. He ate his crumpets and Gentleman's Relish as one who sat on the edge of a volcano, and he called for moral revolution as one who knew there would always be cakes and ale. The dynamic reformer, the Scots Puritan, is immediately apparent in the form of book he wrote and in the largely self-inflicted hardness of his life. The other side, the side that accepted the concrete facts of life and was interested in a wide range of things for their own sake is pervasively, though less explicitly, present. It is there whenever he speaks of England, and whenever he speaks of Shakespeare:

> Shakespeare was not a philosopher or a scientist, but he did have curiosity, he loved the surface of the earth and the process of life—which, it should be repeated, is not the same as wanting to have a good time and stay alive as long as possible.[5]

It is worth comparing with this another passage in which Orwell is speaking of himself; the identification is apparent not only in the general meaning but even in the phraseology:

> So long as I remain alive and well I shall continue to feel strongly about prose style, to love the surface of the earth, and to take a pleasure in solid objects and scraps of useless information.[6]

We may seem to be far away from politics, but the relation becomes clear when we notice another occurrence of the phrase "the process of life," this time in *1984*. O'Brien, a member of the Inner Party, explains that in the future they are building "there will be no curiosity, no enjoyment of the process of life: all competing pleasures will be destroyed."[7]

Politics is the battle that has to be fought so that the non-political life may be lived. Although, as a writer, Orwell is limited by his sense of the politically urgent to a relatively small sector of human experience, one senses that he is not blind to the existence of other, very different, sectors. The limits of his writing are not felt to be the limits of his thought, and, from time to time, remarks slip out which pull the reader up by their sudden broadening of perspective. Thus in a passage devoted to the struggle of the working class throughout the world to raise its standard of living, he suddenly stands outside his subject and says that this would solve nothing in itself; it is merely that privation and brute labour have to be abolished before major problems can be tackled. Then comes a sentence which most of us need to read twice: "The major problem of our time is the decay of the belief in immortality."[8] This remark, one of a few scattered throughout his works which touch on religion, shows that he was not oblivious of the religious impulse or need; which is quite compatible with his anti-clericalism. He never came back to this "major problem"—perhaps because he was too busy fighting the preliminary battle against material hardship

—but the recognition that it existed gave another dimension to that fight.

Whether we describe Orwell as the ordinary man, Tom Bowling, Sancho Panza, infused with a fanatical zeal for truth and justice, or a violent revolutionary saved by his sense of reality, the combination in the one man of apparent but not necessary disparates, is something fundamental to him.

The most usual picture of Orwell is the simplification into the sufferer, the man whose courage and self-sacrifice became almost legendary; after his death he was called a saint, a compliment he would not have understood. The facts on which the legend grew are incontestable, but the descriptions of Orwell which most convince are those where alongside the dedication and the sacrifice, the other side creeps in. Here are the memories of V. S. Pritchett:

> I see a tall, emaciated man with a face scored by the marks of physical suffering. There is the ironic grin of pain at the end of the kind lips and an expression in the fine eyes that had something of the exalted and obstructive far-sightedness one often sees in the blind; an expression that will suddenly become gentle, lazily kind and gleaming with workmanlike humour.[9]

All that has been claimed for Orwell above—the balance, the self-criticism, the humour, even the sense of reality—seems to have gone in his last book, *1984*. For the first time it is possible to suspect him of hysteria. The reason may lie partly in the external circumstances of his life during the last years, and these must now be related. By his own account Orwell had never been very healthy. Though his lung condition was not diagnosed till much later, he traced it to his schooldays when in answer to complaints about his chest he was told to run round the playing-field. His destitute days in Paris and London can have done him little good, but it was after his wound on the Aragon Front that his health got noticeably worse. Tuberculosis was suspected, and the novelist L. H. Myers anonymously provided money for a holiday in North Africa in the winter of 1938–9.[10] During the War, when none of the Services would accept him on medical grounds, he and his wife are said to have regularly drawn less that their rations so as to leave more in the common pool. It may have been as the result of her general run-down condition that his wife died in 1945, after a very minor operation. They had just adopted a baby, and after the publication and success of *Animal Farm*, Orwell was able to go to live in the Hebrides away from London and the pressures which success brought; he took his son and his sister and lived a difficult and exhausting life in a remote farmhouse on the island of Jura. Here, in the worst possible climate, his health grew steadily worse, and here too he must have written the greater part of *1984*. It was finished in a Gloucestershire sanatorium which he was forced to enter in 1949. John Atkins quotes Orwell as saying of the book: "It wouldn't have been so gloomy if I hadn't been so ill."

In fact Orwell recovered enough to leave that sanatorium; he married again, and saw *1984* published. His friends hoped that he might now survive, leading a quiet life with only one lung functioning; a plane had already been chartered to take him to Switzerland when he died suddenly of a haemorrhage in a London hospital on 23 Jan. 1950.

The despair of *1984* is explained but not explained away by Orwell's illness. It had been a perennial feeling of his that human beings are helpless before cruel and gigantic social forces, but against this he had always been able to set his sense of the resilience of ordinary people. What seems to have happened under the strain of illness is that the fears which he had learned to combat by scepticism and self-mocking stoicism were given

ıncritical expression. The tension of the two sides in
)rwell was broken, and the tremendous energy which
vas put into the emotional side cannot entirely compen-
ate us for its loss.

The emotional exaggeration of *1984* is something which
nany readers feel, if only in retrospect; it is something
vhich can, in fact, be traced in the very structure of
he book, and this is worth doing if only as a preliminary
o the more difficult task of explaining why, nevertheless,
t is a book that towers above almost anything else he
vrote, or, indeed almost any novel of our time.

Anyone who has read Orwell's earlier work will
ecognise in *1984* the culmination of all the tendencies
vhich he deplored in his own time. Capitalism has
een replaced, not by democratic Socialism, but by a
ne-party state exercising, in the name of Socialism,
a tyranny more absolute than any known before. It
extends to the control of thought and the annihilation of
objective fact, a possibility Orwell first became aware of
in Spain. The work of the hero, Winston Smith, is in
fact the alteration of references in back numbers of
newspapers to conform with the current Party line; his
heresy is that he still clings to a belief in the evidence of
his senses, that two and two are four, regardless of what
the Party says.

The hysterical devotion of the Party members is a
fully-developed version of the attitudes which Orwell
had discovered among English intellectuals, and castigated in his "Notes on Nationalism." Their cult of power
has in *1984* become the motive force of the whole system.
These developments are all intended to appear as logical
and imminent consequences of present tendencies. A
subversive book, in fact a device of the Party, but which
nevertheless we are clearly intended to accept as true,
describes the history of the twentieth century as one
continuous retrogression. Forced labour, torture, the
transportation of whole peoples, public executions,

imprisonment without trial, all become accepted features of life, and, with the spread of totalitarian political doctrines, are even defended by people who consider themselves progressive. Orwell's reference here to left-wing intellectuals of his generation is pushed home when he adds that the general hardening of outlook set in about 1930.

Orwell presumably set his novel in 1984, only thirty six years on from the time of writing, so as to make the message more urgent. Perhaps his prophecy was more credible then than now, coinciding as it did with the general movement of reaction against the monolithic state, and the penetration to the British public of the realities of police rule, purges, forced confessions and brain-washing in the Soviet Union and Eastern Europe. Nevertheless one must ask whether it was plausible to show the triumph of totalitarian tendencies so completely and over such a short period in English conditions clearly, this is what Orwell wants us to believe had happened, or rather, wants to warn us could happen but he too, whether consciously or not, must have realised the basic implausibility involved, for he introduced, in passing and without emphasis, an event which must be considered not as a mere accelerator of what was already happening, but as a cause in itself. This is a nuclear war, which, it is suggested, occurred sometime in the nineteen-sixties. Anything is credible after a nuclear war, except the assumption that subsequent developments were a natural continuation of tendencies already existing, which is Orwell's general contention.

This is something which hardly interferes with a normal reading of *1984*, but it may have something to do with the feeling of dissatisfaction which the book so often produces. It is one example of how Orwell allowed his sense of urgency to obliterate objections which at another time it was in his character not only to consider out to seek out. In fact, he raised them in an essay on he American writer James Burnham who, incidentally, provided Orwell with the structure used for the world-society of *1984*:

> The slowness of historical change, the fact that any epoch always contains a great deal of the last epoch, is never sufficiently allowed for. Such a manner of thinking is bound to lead to mistaken prophecies, because, even when it gauges the direction of events rightly, it will miscalculate their tempo. . . .
>
> It will be seen that at each point Burnham is predicting *a continuation of the thing that is happening*. Now the tendency to do this is not simply a bad habit, like inaccuracy or exaggeration, which one can correct by taking thought. It is a major mental disease, and its roots lie partly in cowardice and partly in the worship of power, which is not fully separable.[11]

Now Orwell could scarcely be accused of cowardice, nor of admiring power; but he never seems to have been able to overcome a strong feeling that power, synonymous with evil, wins in the end—a perverse form of worship, if you like. This feeling led him, in *1984*, to extrapolate from the present-day situation in the very same way he criticised Burnham for doing.

Power is a word that is always occurring in Orwell, yet it is arguable that it is something he never thought about at length or dispassionately. He never analyses the psychology of power in the individual, or the mechanics of power in the working of institutions. Instead, it is always the cosmic, nightmare force, seen from the point of view of the victim who is suddenly and uncomprehendingly crushed. As the hero of *1984* comes nearer to the centre of power, there is built up the expectation that we shall find the final explanation of this apparently senseless terror. At the beginning he writes in his diary: "I understand How: I do not understand Why." Much later he is about to read the explanation in the book of Goldstein the heretic, but instead falls asleep. When he gets up, it is to be arrested and taken to the cellars of the Ministry of Love. Here, from O'Brien, he finally learns why, and for all the rhetoric it is singularly unconvincing:

> "But always—do not forget this, Winston—always there will be the intoxication of power, constantly increasing and constantly growing subtler. Always, at every moment there will be the thrill of victory, the sensation of trampling on an enemy who is helpless, If you want a picture of the future, imagine a boot trampling on a human face—for ever."[12]

The question we want to ask is the very one that worried Orwell in his essay: "It is curious that in all his talk about the struggle for power Burnham never stops once to ask *why* people want power." The important thing, naturally, is not to refute Orwell out of his own mouth—between 1946, the date of the essay on Burnham, and 1948, he may well have come to agree with the American—but to point out his willingness in *1984* to ignore objections of which he was demonstrably aware, to rely very uncharacteristically on the sheer emotive power of his writing to carry the reader with him. Again it may be that, as in the early novels, Orwell is the victim of the novel-form. He gives himself no opportunity for critical comment on the situations which he lives so painfully from the inside—except in the long extract from the book of Goldstein, and here, significantly, the reader feels relief at the reappearance of sanity and self-control.

When all this has been said, the great strength of the book, its intensity, remains untouched. One is reminded of Orwell's own observation apropos of Swift that "if the force of belief is behind it, a world-view which only ist passes the test of sanity is sufficient to produce a reat work of art." The old commendation of writers 'ho "create a world of their own" is appropriate here. 'he intensity of Orwell's imagination has created a 'orld which, looked at coldly from the outside, may be xaggerated and unlikely: but once in it there is no scape from the nightmare appropriateness of everything. 'he atmosphere is set from the first sentence, with the locks striking thirteen for a utility world of food iortages, rotting houses, clogged drains, shoddy lothes, canteen meals, and eletcricity cuts—the ironic bverse of the Party slogans and the posters showing rong, confident workers striding into the bright iture.

In making the detail of his world credible, the relative loseness of the year 1984 is useful to Orwell. As Richard ierber has pointed out, one of the dangers of literary Jtopias is that they require the insertion of a dis-roportionate amount of circumstantial detail—the nagining of a whole new world.[13] Science, so often the gent of change in Utopias, has in *1984* been restricted to erfecting secret police techniques, and for the rest we ave an approximation to the material conditions of ne Second World War in England. Orwell's accumul-tion of detail can therefore be concentrated in those ectors where it best illustrates his political perception hat totalitarianism cannot tolerate the scope for ndividual development which leisure, brought about by cience, would offer, nor for that matter the empirical vay of thinking which science inculcates. Orwell insists n the squalor and shortages and obscurantism as the ecessary conditions for the propaganda and the state of erpetual hysteria on which the state of Oceania is ased.

Parallel with Winston Smith's ideological heresy of elieving in objective truth, ascertainable by the senses, uns his secret love affair with Julia, another worker in

the Ministry of Truth. It is secret because illegal, an
illegal because the Party cannot allow the creation o
intimate worlds outside its own world of mass emotion
Marriage has to be accepted as an unfortunately sti
necessary institution, but mutual physical love, wheth
inside or outside marriage, is regarded as a crim
Richard Rees considers that one of Orwell's limitatio
was a lack of interest in psychology, and it is certainl
true that he was too concerned with the concrete wor
to explore Proustian labyrinths of the mind for the
own sake. But he had always been fascinated by th
private reasons for public attitudes, what made peopl
martyrs or pacifists or socialists, or why dogmat
extremists were able so easily to switch to other extreme
There is a terrible logic in the policy which makes th
love affair of Winston and Julia criminal. Julia explai
why the Party cannot tolerate it:

> "When you make love you're using up energy; and afterwards you feel happy and don't give a damn for anything. They can't bear you to feel like that. They want you to be bursting with energy all the time. All this marching up and down and cheering and waving flags is simply sex gone sour. If you're happy inside yourself, why should you get excited about Big Brother and the Two Minutes Hate and all the rest of their bloody rot?"[14]

Before he first spoke to her, Winston had drean
about Julia. In that dream she had come walkin
towards him across a field and with a single moveme
torn off her clothes and flung them aside. It was n
desire that Winston felt, but admiration for a gestu
which "with its grace and carelessness seemed t
annihilate a whole culture." Winston, we are tol
woke up with the word Shakespeare on his lips. This
less surprising when we remember that Shakespeare, f
Orwell, is above all associated with enjoyment of th

"process of life," for which the Party has no place in its scheme.

It is characteristic that this snatch of beauty should come in a dream; for everything that Orwell prized in his own time is shown in *1984* as some frail, precious remnant or memory of a lost order. There is probably a greater sense of beauty in *1984* than in anything Orwell ever wrote, but throughout it is expressed in an elegiac strain.

On several occasions Winston dreams about his mother, or remembers some incident from his childhood, often with feelings of guilt or self-reproach. His mother stands for the simple absolute virtues of family life—love, loyalty, self-sacrifice, emotions that have depth and dignity and which the Party has replaced by strident public emotions. He remembers the gesture of his mother's arm bent protectively round his sister, and this gesture is repeated in a war-film which he goes to see. An enemy ship has been bombed and a middle-aged woman is seen sitting in a lifeboat full of children, her arms round a little boy. The Party members in the cinema applaud as an Oceanian helicopter plants a bomb right in the centre of the children. The Party has no feelings (as these were understood by Winston's mother), and since it is all-powerful, such feelings can be said to have disappeared, except in the case of Winston who has his memories and his relationship with Julia, itself a survival from a past age:

> He wondered vaguely whether in the abolished past it had been a normal experience to lie in bed like this, in the cool of a summer evening, a man and a woman with no clothes on, making love when they chose, talking of what they chose, not feeling any compulsion to get up, simply lying there and listening to the peaceful sounds outside. Surely there could never have been a time when that seemed ordinary?[15]

It is the evidence of their senses which they can hardly bring themselves to believe, Their senses, their bodies, confirm that a different sort of world once existed, and it is because they are a further confirmation that things have not always been as they are now that Winston values the odd concrete fragments of the past which he comes across—an old writing-book with good quality paper and a paperweight of rainwater glass with a piece of coral at the centre, both of which he buys from the old-fashioned keeper of a derelict antique-shop. They form the elegiac accompaniment to the doomed love of Winston and Julia, and their small world of physical touch and human feeling, banished from the greater world constructed by the Party, is reduced to the size and fragility of the paperweight:

> It was as though the surface of the glass had been the arch of the sky, enclosing a tiny world with its atmosphere complete. He had the feeling that he could get inside it, and that in fact he was inside it, along with the mahogany bed and the gateleg table, and the clock and the steel engraving and the paperweight itself. The paperweight was the room he was in, and the coral was Julia's life and his own, fixed in a sort of eternity at the heart of the crystal.[16]

Part of the lyrical strain are the "proles," the lowest order in the state, who are kept so far below political consciousness that they can be left free of the rigid surveillance which Party members undergo, and also free of the conditioning to hate. At the filmshow mentioned above it is a prole woman who gets up and shouts "they didn't oughter of showed it not in front of the kids." Decency is still to be found in the working class; the proles grow up and wither like leaves on the tree, and on their indestructibility Winston bases his hopes of future change, though it be thousands of years away. Like the cart-horse which gave Orwell the idea for

Animal Farm, they are unconscious of their strength, and unlikely to become conscious within any foreseeable period of time. Winston writes in his diary: "Until they become conscious they will never rebel, and until they have rebelled they cannot become conscious."

These words are a more or less transposed version of Arthur Koestler's phrase which Orwell quoted in his essay on that writer: "Without education of the masses, no social progress; without social progress, no education of the masses." Orwell goes on to make a criticism of Koestler which is directly relevant to Winston in *1984*. He describes him as a disillusioned hedonist, who because no revolution brings about the earthly paradise, considers all such movements equal failures, and yet preserves a long-term optimism that by some process which cannot be envisaged in political terms, things will eventually turn out well. This is roughly Winston's position. His actual encounters with the proles offer him no hope. A small group of men arguing fiercely in the street, are, he finds, only contradicting each other about the lottery, and an old man whom he takes for a drink in the hope that he will provide some coherent evidence of what life was like before the Revolution, remembers only useless fragments of his private life. Yet Winston believes that one day the proles will rise up, and that then no power will be able to stop them.

For Orwell, however, such a doubtful and distant hope was too close to despair. Even while he is thinking all this, Winston is being watched by the Thought Police. The act of faith in a distant, future change for the good, the hope at the end of Shelley's *Prometheus Unbound*, or even Hardy's *Dynasts*, was not possible for Orwell. Perhaps it requires a poetic exaltation which can only be achieved by removing the eye momentarily from the spectacle of suffering.

The proles are not a hope, but they are part of the elegiac strain, the feeling for a potential which might

once have been developed, before mechanisation an
education were turned into weapons of oppression, no
of liberation. The working class have been made int
animals, and like animals have the naive, patheti
beauty of the strong but powerless. On the afternoo
before their arrest, at the window of the room ove
the antique shop, Julia and Winston watch a hug
prole woman pegging nappies in the cobbled yar
below:

> The woman down there had no mind, she had only strong arms, a warm heart, and a fertile belly. He wondered how many children she had given birth to. It might easily be fifteen. She had had her momentary flowering, a year, perhaps, of wild-rose beauty, and then she had swollen like a fertilized fruit and grown hard and red and coarse, and then her life had been laundering, scrubbing, darning, cooking, sweeping, polishing, mending, scrubbing, laundering, first for children, then for grand-children, over thirty unbroken years. At the end of it she was still singing. The mystical reverence that he felt for her was somehow mixed up with the aspect of the pale, cloudless sky, stretching away behind the chimney pots into interminable distance. . . . The birds sang, the proles sang, the Party did not sing. All round the world, in London and New York, in Africa and Brazil, and in the mysterious, forbidden lands beyond the frontiers, in the streets of Paris and Berlin, in the villages of the endless Russian plain, in the bazaars of China and Japan—everywhere stood the same solid unconquerable figures, made monstrous by work and childbearing, toiling from birth to death and still singing.[17]

The tenderness of this passage hardly squares with th
view which sees Orwell's life as a long love-affair wit
the working class, and *1984* as the disillusionment. I

was always for its potential, for its residual incorruptibility that he had valued it. Winston, believing that there would at some time be a future which belonged to the proles, believed that it was also one which the true intellectual could share "if you kept alive the mind as they kept alive the body, and passed on the secret doctrine that two plus two make four."[18] Winston, in trying to see the world as it is on the evidence of his senses, is the last representative of the intellectual tradition in which Orwell placed himself, a tradition which sees the interest of the oppressed as the true interest of the intellectual, "for where there is equality there can be sanity."

It is disillusion with the intellectual movements of his own generation that lies behind *1984*. Orwell felt that the very people who should have been defending truth and intellectual freedom were giving themselves uncritically to ideologies whose only justification was power. Like this they condemned themselves to unreality ("doublethink" in 1984 terminology) and at the same time betrayed the uneducated whose protectors they should have been. The terrible pity of this betrayal is brought out in one of Winston's memories of early childhood, when he was taken to a tube station to shelter from what may have been a nuclear raid, and saw an old man weeping:

> In his childish way Winston grasped that some terrible thing, something which was beyond forgiveness and could never be remedied, had just happened. It also seemed to him that he knew what it was. Someone whom the old man loved.—a little granddaughter, perhaps—had been killed. Every few minutes the old man kept repeating,
>
> "We didn't ought to have trusted 'em. I said so, Ma, didn't I? That's what comes of trusting 'em I said so all along. We didn't ought to 'ave trusted the buggers."

But which buggers they didn't ought to have trusted Winston could not now remember.[19]

In the third part of *1984* the elegiac *motif* has gone; there is not even the shadow or memory of hope. Nightmare closes in as Winston, separated from Julia, faces a succession of tortures in the cellars of the Ministry of Love. The final horror, when Winston, confronted with his secret terror, rats, which are to be allowed to gnaw his face, cries out "Do it to Julia," is rather too heightened and at the same time too arranged for most people. It was no doubt essential to Orwell's purpose to show that power was not only an obsession in the mind, but was bound to rest, at base, on the use of physical force; the question is whether he defeats his purpose by the exaggeration of horror. Individual reactions seem to differ here. For some people this section of the book is too painful to read, while for others it has already crossed the line beyond which the reader finds his own sense of the ridiculous intruding.

If this part of the book sticks in the mind it is because it is true not to any reality known in Britain, but to deep and widespread fears. It is a nightmare, but a nightmare appropriate to our age. The steel-shod guards, the cellars of the secret police where the daylight never shines, the beatings-up, the refinements of torture with electric terminals and hypodermics; the passionless white-coated men in the background preparing the unknown, excruciating pain, the loving-cruel face of the inquisitor—this is the modern scene of suffering, realised so forcefully, and entirely from the victim's point of view, by Orwell that his book has become what few books become, a major influence, even indirectly on people who have never read it.

Outside Britain not only have the physical horrors been more familiar: the mental atmosphere has not seemed so fantastic. Czeslaw Milosz, a Polish intellectual writing of the Stalinist period says: "Even those who know Orwell only by hearsay are amazed that a writer who never lived in Russia should have such a keen perception into its life."[20] In those days in Poland *1984* was a rare and dangerous book, rather like Goldstein's book, and known only to the Inner Party.

We do not know how and to what extent books really affect our attitudes, but it is at least possible that they do so more by their emotional charge than by intellectual argument. It may be that *1984* is not an effective warning, taking this to mean an intellectual demonstration of what will happen if we continue on our course, but that it has had a greater effect by strengthening at the level of our prejudices and fears, our resistance to political myths, mass suggestion and all propaganda. If, as Orwell says "the energy that actually shapes the world springs from emotions—racial pride, leader-worship, religious belief, love of war—"[21] then perhaps these cannot be withstood by mere liberal principle, but only by the creation of another emotion—fear.

Isaac Deutscher has drawn attention to the similarities between *1984* and Zamyatin's *We*. When Orwell himself reviewed a translation of that book in *Tribune*, apart from noticing various technological features of the police state, which were later to be useful to him, he praised Zamyatin for his intuitive grasp of the irrational side of totalitarianism which in his view made the book superior to Huxley's *Brave New World*. It is a possible defence of *1984* that the lack of proportion, the irrationality, are inherent in the subject-matter it treats.

And yet—and yet, anyone who has sympathised with Orwell's earlier work must feel a falling-off in *1984*—not of intensity, and certainly not of courage, but of zest, of that liveliness and resilience which makes even the sad story of *Animal Farm* something to remember with pleasure. Above all it is a falling-off from his mood in

Spain, commemorated in the lines which mark the uppe
limit of his faith:

> No bomb that ever burst
> Shatters the crystal spirit[22]

The same symbolic crystal is there in the paperweigh
of *1984*, but the faith has gone. It is the moment afte
the police arrive to arrest Julia and Winston.

> There was another crash. Someone had picked up the glass paperweight and smashed it to pieces on the hearth-stone.
>
> The fragment of coral, a tiny crinkle of pink like a sugar rosebud from a cake, rolled across the mat. How small, thought Winston, how small it always was![23]

Throughout this book, Orwell has been explained i
terms of polarities held in a tension: the partisan an
the recorder of objective truth, the conservative and th
revolutionary, the romantic idealist and the down-to
earth sceptic. On the stylistic plane it was the emotiona
rhythm, the rhetoric of his prose, in tension with catalo
gues of detailed facts. The method is perhaps inevitable
and it is all the more important to insist that mor
characteristic than the polarities is the Orwellian tensio
itself. The sad thing about *1984* is that the same element
are present as in the earlier Orwell: but the tension i
gone. His fears are now dominant and his hopes hav
turned into a lyrical lament for something already lost
The question now arises whether it was not implicit i
the Orwellian tension that it should break down, whethe
he was not right when he wrote in *The Road to Wigan Pie*
that "it is impossible to be honest and to remain alive."
It may be that the habit of insisting on ascertainabl
truths, while admirable in the method of a critic o

historian is inadequate for coming to terms with one's own existence where, in the absence of possible proof to our senses, some hypothesis must be allowed to stand. As a revolutionary, that is, someone who believed in and worked for a great change in society, Orwell was brought to face the likelihood that what he wanted to happen was not going to happen. Other people faced with the same realisation have escaped into disillusioned reaction—come to believe that people do not really change and that revolutions are frauds—or, alternatively into a transcendental faith in the future. One can persuade oneself, in fact, either that what one previously thought was going to happen is no longer desirable, or that what one wants to happen will eventually happen, even against all current probability. Orwell did neither; he saw the world moving in one direction when he passionately wanted it to move in the other. It is a pity that *1984* was his last word, for the courage displayed there would also have been a courage to go on.

It seems that there was a way on in Orwell's mind. Several of his friends mention that just before his death he had been re-reading Conrad's political novels. Paul Potts even holds that Orwell completed an essay on the subject which may linger in the files of some small magazine that had to cease publication. A short appreciation which *was* published in a London Polish newspaper shows that Orwell particularly admired the detached position of Conrad in such books as *Nostromo*, *The Secret Agent*, and *Under Western Eyes*. "He had a sort of grown-upness and political understanding which would have been almost impossible to a native English writer at that time."[24] Conrad's novels about anarchism at the turn of the century would naturally have been fascinating for Orwell. Through them he could investigate the early period of the totalitarian movements and the dilemma of moral purists thrown into the arena of political action. He had already touched on the subject in his essay on Tolstoy:

> The distinction that really matters is not between violence and non-violence, but between having and not having the appetite for power. There are people who are convinced of the wickedness both of armies and of police forces, but who are nevertheless much more intolerant and inquisitorial in outlook than the normal person who believes that it is necessary to use violence in certain circumstances, They will not say to somebody else, "Do this, that and the other or you will go to prison," but they will, if they can, get inside his brain and dictate his thoughts for him in the minutest particulars. Creeds like pacifism and anarchism, which seem on the surface to imply a complete renunciation of power, rather encourage this habit of mind.[25]

To say that this was the way on for Orwell must, of course, be speculative, but to suggest that he would have found some further analysis of the complexity of the moral world, some other tension to recognise, seems very probable from everything that went before. The impression given by *1984* of final heroic defeat, is too convenient a distortion: but neither is there evidence for thinking that his death robbed us of a prophet. He was at the same time too limited in imagination and too sane for this; he never soared so high as, say, D. H. Lawrence, but he never ranged so far from demonstrable truth. He had the virtues and limitations of the permanent exile, who, in Raymond Williams's words "sees the inadequacies of the groups he is rejecting; but where, in himself, is the final ground of truth?"[26] Orwell offers no final ground, and therefore can have no ideological following, though he has a personal one. He was not a moral teacher but a moral perceiver, nd to understand him is not to ask how he would ave solved a problem, but how he would have seen it.

REFERENCES

1. *World Review*, Jun. 1950.
2. Paul Potts, *Dante Called you Beatrice*, 1960, p. 72.
3. *E.Y.E.*, p. 12.
4. John Raymond, "The Barrack-room Lawyer."
5. *S.A.E.*, p. 5.
6. *E.Y.E.*, p. 14.
7. *1984*, p. 273.
8. *E.Y.E.*, p. 174.
9. V. S. Pritchett in *New Statesman*, 28 Jan., 1950.
0. Richard Rees, *Fugitive from the Camp of Victory*, p. 75.
1. *S.A.E.*, p. 151.
2. *1984*, p. 273.
13. Richard Gerber, *Utopian Fantasy*, 1955, p. 121 ff.
14. *1984*, p. 137.
15. *1984*, p. 148.
16. *1984*, p. 151.
17. *1984*, p. 225.
18. *1984*, p. 227.
19. *1984*, p. 36.
20. Czeslaw Milosz, *The Captive Mind*, 1953, p. 42.
21. *C.E.*, p. 94.
22. *E.Y.E.*, p. 176.
23. *1984*, p. 229.
24. *Wiadomosci*, 10 Apr., 1949.
25. *S.A.E.*, p.54.
26. *Essays in Criticism*, 1955, p. 51.

CHAPTER VIII

ORWELL AND THE ENGLISH LANGUAGE

In this chapter we shall chiefly be concerned wit
Orwell's essays; these have been touched on separatel
according to their subject, and this may have suggeste
for them a minor position in the body of his work. If so
this is the place to express the opinion that, taken to
gether, they stand in the first rank alongside *Animal Farm*
One of the reasons for their success is that they sho
Orwell's language at its best. Whether literary o
political, they are critical essays, and Orwell's interes
in language was a critical interest. This is best illustrate
by Sir Richard Rees's anecdote of Orwell's reply whe
told that under Socialism there would be no feeling o
being at the mercy of unpredictable and irresponsibl
powers: "I notice people always say 'under Socialism'."
His concern with language was inseparable from hi
concern with politics; or rather, both grew from hi
belief in the existence of objective and discoverabl
truths. Dishonesty in politics and dishonesty in languag
were the concealment of these truths. When he criticise
an inflated, Latinate, highly-abstract style, it is the injur
to truth and therefore to the cause of humanity whic
he resents:

> Defenceless villages are bombarded from the air, the inhabitants driven out into the countryside, the cattle machine-gunned, the huts set on fire with incendiary bullets: this is called *pacification*. Millions of peasants are robbed of their farms and sent trudging along the roads with no more than they can carry: this is called *transfer of population* or *rectification of frontiers*.[1]

In *1984*, dishonesty has been institutionalised, and an unreal language, Newspeak, has been developed to express the world-view and mental habits of Oceanian society, and at the same time to make impossible other ways of thinking. The ultimate aim, not yet achieved in *1984*, was that heretical thoughts should become unthinkable, or at least inexpressible in language. The principles and practice of Newspeak as described in Orwell's Appendix to *1984* are ingenious and amusing, though the psychological and philosophical basis of the whole system does not bear looking at too closely; the value of the Appendix is rather that it draws together Orwell's many sensitive perceptions about the English of his own time, For instance we are told that the practice of using abbreviations for political organisations was at first adopted instinctively, but that later the value of the habit was recognised, so that it became a conscious policy in Newspeak. Abbreviations narrowed the field of association:

> The words *Communist International*, for instance, call up a composite picture of universal human brotherhood, red flags, barricades, Karl Marx, and the Paris Commune. The word *Comintern*, on the other hand, suggests merely a tightly-knit organisation and a well-defined body of doctrine.[2]

For Orwell, the great defence against confusion and dishonesty is experience with the senses, expressed in language by the concrete and the simple word. His advice is to think as far as possible in terms of pictures and sensations and then to look for the word that best expresses the meaning you have formulated wordlessly. To put the sensations first was his own method, as we observed in the case of "Shooting an Elephant." Another example is his essay "Looking Back on the Spanish Civil War," where the initial sentence reads: "First of all the physical memories, the sounds, the smells and

the surfaces of things." It is a good method as Orwel
uses it, and for his purpose, which is to draw mora
perceptions from personal experience. But how woul
it apply to more complex or technical subject-matter
One wonders whether Orwell is not implicitly attackin
certain types of subject-matter as much as the abstrac
manner of writing; whether he is not in fact suggestin
that nothing is worth saying that cannot be said i
language that is simple, concrete, and passionate. It is
in fact, a manifestation in another field of the belief tha
the moral impulse to change counted for more than th
methods:

> It seemed to me then—it seems to me now, for that matter—that economic injustice will stop the moment we want it to stop, and no sooner, and if we genuinely want it to stop the method adopted hardly matters.[3]

This integrity between what Orwell thought abou
language and what he thought about life can be foun
throughout his essay "Politics and the English Lan
guage." There he describes what he means by
"defending" the English language, and the argument
and even the phraseology run closely parallel with th
passage in *The Lion and the Unicorn* where he proclaim
that patriotism has nothing to do with conservatism
Defending the language, he says, has nothing to do wit
archaism, or with correct grammar, or the avoidance o
Americanisms, or what is called "a good prose style.'
What defending the language means to Orwell is makin
one's meaning clear, conserving the capacity of th
language to express clear thought. "Good prose is like a
window-pane."

When Orwell writes about the use of language, he is
thinking of prose, and of what we can call critical prose
indeed he believed that the prose tradition as we know
it was the product of the Protestant centuries, and
inextricably linked with individual, independen

ıought. Some poetry might express the feelings of a
·hole group, but good prose was the creation of, and
ore the stamp of, the individual mind. The threat to
ıdependent thinking came in the form of package
leologies, expressed in pre-fabricated phrases which in
me came to corrupt the language. No one, he believed,
ould wholly avoid dishonest jargon in political writing,
nce this was bound up with the corruption of politics
self. But he did think, like Dr Johnson, that we could
alliate what we could not cure, and make a start at
utting things right from the verbal end.

In his essay "Politics and the English Language,"
e gave a number of rules for use where instinct failed.
ome of these make useful standards by which to measure
)rwell's own practice. "Never use a metaphor, simile or
ther figure of speech which you are used to seeing in
rint." This is not just a simple warning against clichés;
)rwell in fact was quite fond of conversational clichés,
nd further on in the essay he defends dead metaphors,
nd takes care to distinguish them from dying metaphors.
Iis concern is not originality of expression, and dead
netaphors, if they express a clear meaning are as
cceptable as any other words; indeed the language is
ırgely made up of them. But the dying metaphor is a
hrase which is used loosely and done to death because
t still carries some small emotional charge, and the writer
vants to use this to browbeat or impress the reader
n a general way instead of expressing his meaning
learly.

"If it is possible to cut a word out, always cut it out."
This sounds an obvious piece of good advice, and yet
)rwell does not follow it himself. His style, though it
arefully avoids decorative words, which is probably
vhat he had in mind when formulating the rule, is not
onsistently terse, but has a ballast of those repetitions
vhich make for clarity in speech, but can be omitted in
vriting. In the passage quoted on page 102, we see this

in the strictly unneccessary repetition of the infiniti "stop" throughout. It gives a balance and a force t the expression, of a rather different kind from th achieved by epigrammatic concision. Orwell's mann is a form of directness rather than of cleverness.

Orwell's special excellence, which we are no considering, is something that has to be analysed in h practice. His own writing on the English language critical and does not help us to understand the positiv merits of his method. The chief of these seems to lie i the inspired use of appropriate rhetorical forms, an indeed their conscious use. The latter point is difficult t demonstrate conclusively, since Orwell never mentio this aspect of his work, but given the number of rhetoric borrowings, and their controlled adaptation to his pu pose, it can hardly be doubted. It is interesting th Orwell expressed great admiration for the individua hard-hitting, and concrete writing of the Elizabetha pamphleteers, whose use of rhetorical forms is so fund mental to their success.

What we are concerned with are the dynamic pattern of phrase, both rhythmic and syntactic, which conve not so much the writer's logical meaning as the emotion line and direction of his thought; the element in h writing which (in the original meaning of rhetorica influences and persuades the reader. These forms go o being used, of course, though literary criticism h unfortunately lost the terms for discussing them. The are perhaps of greatest use to writers themselves, an the case for analysing and categorising them rather tha merely working by instinct, is that, while this ca never insure that they will be used well, bringing the into the conscious field will make possible their controlle use—one might add, their artistic use.

The rhetoric can be anything from the generalise tone, which sets up the reader's relationship with th author, to set patterns of phrase taken from othe authors who have used them effectively. Thus, in the passage quoted earlier in this chapter, the repeated phrase "this is called pacification," "this is called transfer of population," is taken straight from Swift, and has the same satiric effect.

The base from which Orwell's special effects rise is the general and dispersed conversational effect touched on earlier. This is not intended to mean that his manner is undemanding and slack, nor that it is in the tradition of English essay-writing, relaxedly elegant, charming, and easy on the mind. It is rather that Orwell, above all in his essays, gives the impression of the speaking voice—but the voice of a man speaking thoughtfully, and deliberately, and directly. That he thought in terms of the speaking voice is evident on almost any page of the essays from his use of italics for emphasis: "Kipling *is* a jingo imperialist," "It is quite possible that man's major problems will *never* be solved," or "The Houyhnhnms, we are told, were unanimous on almost all subjects. The only question they ever *discussed* was how to deal with the Yahoos." The italicised words are direct in two ways. First, this is usually the quickest way of saying the thing; and secondly, the same meaning would otherwise have to be conveyed by a more literary and artificial arrangement of the sentence, bringing out emphasis by position.

Another illustration of his conversational directness can be found in these two openings to his essays, where the first words brush aside academic preliminaries, bringing us straight into the subject:

> Most people who bother with the matter at all would admit that the English language is in a bad way.[4]

> Somewhere or other Byron makes use of the French word *longueur*, and remarks in passing that though in England we happen not to have the *word*, we have the *thing* in profusion. In the same way . . .[5]

The conversational tone in Orwell is very much a question of colloquial turns of phrase, not used for picaresque effect, but because they are direct and have the personal ring—phrases such as "at any rate to my ear," or "as I understand it," "for that matter," or "come to think of it."

The conversational manner gives Orwell the ease of transition which is possible in speech, frees him from that striving after formal and often unreal connexions, the inevitable "howevers" and "neverthelesses" of a more literary style. The colloquial tone was particularly useful when it came to polemics; it permitted him, without suddenly jarring the reader, to use vulgarisms which are more vital than any conceivable literary equivalents. So when Orwell says "bum-suckers," or "kiss the arse of," or "smelly little orthodoxies," the phrases come fairly naturally out of his ground-style of colloquialism; in a more literary style, they would sound self conscious and palpably designed to shock.

It is his polemical talent that makes Orwell so readable. He enjoyed, and the reader enjoys, the smashing epithet or the quiet satiric undermining of the enemy. Dali's autobiography is "a strip-tease act conducted in pink limelight," "Poetry on the air sounds like the Muses in striped trousers," or take this passage satirising the sentimentality of Dickens:

> The ideal to be striven after, then, appears to be something like this; a hundred thousand-pounds, a quaint old house with plenty of ivy on it, a sweet womanly wife, a horde of children, and no work. Everything is safe, soft, peaceful and, above all, domestic. In the moss-grown churchyard down the road are the graves of the loved ones who passed away before the happy ending happened. The servants are comic and feudal, the children prattle round your feet, the old friends sit at your fireside, talking of past

days, there is the endless succession of enormous meals, the cold punch and sherry negus, the feather beds and warming-pans, the Christmas parties with charades and blind man's buff; but nothing ever happens, except the yearly childbirth.[6]

One of Orwell's favourite devices was a sort of grand slam at a whole collection of enemies, insulting them directly, and then again indirectly by the act of association. The names in this example are a little dated, but the insult still comes through:

> When one thinks of all the people who support or have supported Fascism, one stands amazed at their diversity. What a crew! Think of a programme which at any rate for a while could bring Hitler, Petain, Montague Norman, Pavelitch, William Randolph Hearst, Streicher, Buchman, Ezra Pound, Juan March, Cocteau, Thyssen, Father Coughlin, the mufti of Jerusalem, Arnold Lunn, Antonescu, Spengler, Beverley Nichols, Lady Houston and Marinetti all into the same boat. But the clue is really very simple. They are all people with something to lose, or people who long for a hierarchical society and dread the prospect of a world of free and equal human beings.[7]

Now this is the very method Swift uses at the end of *Gulliver's Travels*. Orwell noted that passage in his essay on Swift, and there he asks whether this device does not reflect "the irresponsible violence of the powerless." At first sight the criticism might seem easily transferred to Orwell's own catalogue of villains: but in fact there is an important difference. Swift assembles every example of human folly and vice to make an indiscriminate assault on humanity as a whole. Orwell's list has a much more specific common factor which he makes clear in the last sentence of the quoted passage.

He has taken the form from Swift but is using it differently, to establish a moral category of his own, cutting across the conventional divisions. It is in fact a rhetorical weapon against party lines, a mould for his independent judgment.

But the stylistic form which is, perhaps, most characteristically Orwellian is the one which reflects the double standard mentioned earlier, of the political activist on the one hand, and on the other the impartial observer. Orwell had to reconcile his wish to persuade and move people in a particular direction with his respect for truth and his sense of fairness; he did it by developing a special manner of expression: first he strikes the main blow with all the force he is capable of, and only then, when the blow has gone home, does he qualify the statement. Here are two examples:

> If you look for the working classes in fiction, and especially English fiction, all you find is a hole. This statement needs qualifying.[8]

> A thing that strikes one when one looks below the surface of Dickens's books is that, as nineteenth-century novelists go, he is rather ignorant. He knows very little about the way things really happen. At first sight this statement looks flatly untrue and it needs some qualification.[9]

It may seem a small matter whether an author qualifies his meaning by means of "perhaps" in the main clause rather than by adding a second, modifying clause or sentence. The logical meaning may amount to very much the same thing. But the tone is altogether different, reflecting the difference between those for whom writing is a form of intellectual exercise and those, like Orwell, for whom it is a form of action. Orwell's first questions to himself are: what is the propagandist purpose, what do I want to persuade people of, and how can it best be done? Secondly, not in absolute importance, but in strategic relevance: is this statement wholly true and fair? It is a way of thinking, and a very Orwellian one, crystallised in a way of expression that is also typically Orwellian. The same honesty is repeated on the scale of a whole book in *Homage to Catalonia*, where, after pages of strong partisan argument intended to move the reader to sympathy, he feels bound to add:

> In case I have not said this somewhere earlier in the book I will say it now: beware of my partisanship, my mistakes of fact and the distortion inevitably caused by my having seen only one corner of events. And beware of exactly the same things when you read any other book on this period of the Spanish war.[10]

The idea of confessing bias as the best means of reaching impartiality, is one that recurs in Orwell, and it is very probable that he got it from Chesterton's *The Victorian Age in Literature*. This illustrates nicely the extent and limits of literary and stylistic influences on Orwell. Where he found an idea that attracted him, he took it over, more often than not with some echo of the original expression, since for him the meaning was not easily separated from the way of saying it. Chesterton was rich in ideas and expressions that interested Orwell, but he was less honest, and when Orwell takes his idea of confessing bias, he uses if differently. Chesterton does it to disarm criticism, Orwell to encourage a critical mentality in the reader.

Swift and Chesterton were obvious quarries for a polemic writer, and their influence is the most easily traced in Orwell's turns of phrase. But he also took over the expression of certain moods from more descriptive writers, where he felt they had seized some feeling of his own. He did not, of course, plagiarise; the relation is subtler and would need very extensive quotation to illustrate. But no one who reads, in their context, the

Professor's thoughts in Conrad's *The Secret Agent*,[11] and then Winston's meditation on the proles quoted on page 92, can miss the affinity of thought and tone.

Just as Orwell repeats the right word or tone where he finds it in another author, so he repeats phrases within his own writing; the words "the process of life" as we have seen, stand for something basic in his thinking. Having found the words which best express his meaning, he sticks to them, for they are the proof that the thing exists. The concrete object, the personal experience, these are the foundations of the truth, and the linguistic expression of those truths have only to be found. Newspeak was the language of a world-view; Orwell's language aimed to reflect a world which, he never doubted, is what it is.

REFERENCES

1. *S.A.E.*, p. 96.
2. *1984*, p. 313.
3. *R.W.P.*, p. 150.
4. *S.A.E.*, p. 84.
5. *E.Y.E.*, p. 41.
6. *C.E.*, p. 44.
7. *E.Y.E.*, p. 173.
8. *C.E.*, p. 3.
9. *C.E.*, p. 35.
10. *H.T.C.*, p. 247.
11. Joseph Conrad, *The Secret Agent*, New Collected Edition, pp. 81–2.

BIBLIOGRAPHY

As this volume came up for reprinting (1968) Secker & Warburg announced the forthcoming publication of *Collected Essays, Journalism, and Letters of George Orwell* in four volumes. These will present a far more extensive view of Orwell's prose than has hitherto been possible, rendering section (e) of this bibliography obsolete. The titles are Vol. I, *An Age Like This, 1920-1940*; Vol. II, *My Country Right or Left, 1940-1943*; Vol. III, *As I Please, 1943-45*; and Vol. IV, *In Front of Your Nose, 1945-50*.

ZEKE, ZOLTANG and WILLIAM WHITE: "George Orwell—a Selected Bibliography," in *Bulletin of Bibliography*, Boston, Mass. May-Aug. 1961.

——: "Orwelliana: A Checklist," in *Bulletin of Bibliography*, Sept.-Dec. 1961 and Jan.-Apr. 1962.

McDOWELL, JENNIFER: "George Orwell: Bibliographical Addenda," in *Bulletin of Bibliography*, Jan.-Apr., May-Aug. and Sept.-Dec. 1963.

I. GEORGE ORWELL

(a) Novels

Burmese Days. New York (Harper) * London 1949.

A Clergyman's Daughter. London (Gollancz) 1935. * London 1960.

Keep the Aspidistra Flying. London (Gollancz) 1936. * London 1954.

Coming up for Air. London (Gollancz) 1939. * London 1954.

Animal Farm. * London 1945. Ukrainian edition with Preface by Orwell 1947.

1984 * London 1949.

(b) Autobiography

Down and Out in Paris and London. London (Secker & Warburg) 1935. * London 1949.

The Road to Wigan Pier. Left Book Club edition, with Foreword by Victor Gollancz London (Gollancz) 1937. * London 1959.

Homage to Catalonia. London (Secker & Warburg) 1938. * London 1951.

(c) Pamphlets

The Lion and the Unicorn. London (Secker & Warburg) 1941. * London 1962.

James Burnham and the Managerial Revolution. London 1946.

(*d*) *Volumes of Essays*

Inside the Whale. London (Gollancz) 1940.

Critical Essays. London (Secker & Warburg) 1946. * Reset edition London 1951. ("Charles Dickens" 1939; "Boys' Weeklies" 1939; "Wells, Hitler and the World State" 1941; "The Art of Donald McGill" 1941; "Rudyard Kipling" 1942; "W. B. Yeats" 1943; "Benefit of Clergy: Some Notes on Salvador Dali" 1944; "Arthur Koestler" 1944; "Raffles and Miss Blandish" 1944; "In Defence of P. G. Wodehouse" 1945.)

Shooting an Elephant. * London 1950. ("A Hanging" 1931; "Shooting an Elephant" 1936; "How the Poor Die" 1946; "The Prevention of Literature" 1946; " Politics and the English Language" 1946; "Politics vs. Literature: An Examination of Gulliver's Travels" 1946; "Second Thoughts on James Burnham" 1946; "Reflections on Gandhi" 1947; "Lear, Tolstoy and the Fool" 1947; "I Write as I Please"; extracts dealing with various subjects which appeared in *Tribune* from 1945 on).

Such, Such were the Joys. New York (Harcourt, Brace) 1953. (Contents are the same as *England Your England* except for the omission of two extracts from *The Road to Wigan Pier* and the insertion of the title essay, printed here for the first time.)

England Your England. London (Secker & Warburg) 1953. ("Inside the Whale" 1940; "Looking Back on the Spanish War" 1943; "Marrakech" 1939; "Anti-Semitism in Britain" 1945; "Poetry and the Microphone" 1945; "Notes on Nationalism" 1945; "Why I Write" 1947; "Writers and Leviathan" 1948. The volume also includes two excerpts from *The Road to Wigan Pier* under the titles "North and South" and "Down the Mine" and the first section of *The Lion and the Unicorn* under the title *England Your England*.)

Collected Essays. London (Secker & Warburg) 1961. Collects the essays contained in *Shooting an Elephant, Critical Essays,* and *England Your England* but omits "Rudyard Kipling," "Reflections on Gandhi," the pieces assembled under the title "I Write as I please," and the extracts from *The Road to Wigan Pier* and *The Lion and the Unicorn* included in *England Your England*.

(*e*) *Miscellaneous*

Betrayal of the Left. London (Gollancz) 1941. Contribution by George Orwell.

Victory or Vested Interests? London (Routledge) 1942. Contribution by George Orwell.

"T. S. Eliot." Article by George Orwell collected in *Little Reviews Anthology*. London (G. Allen) 1943.

Talking to India. London (G. Allen) 1943. Contribution by George Orwell.

Love of Life by Jack London. London (Elek Books) 1946. Preface by George Orwell.

"Freedom and Happiness." Review of Zamyatins *We* in *Tribune*, 4 Jan. 1946.

The English People. (Britain in Pictures series) London (Collins) 1947. Text by George Orwell.

British Pamphleteers (VOL I). London (Wingate) 1948. Introduction.

"Conrad's place and rank in English Letters." Short contribution by George Orwell to the symposium in the Polish weekly *Wiadomosci* (London), 10 Apr. 1949.

World Review, June 1950. Contains selections from George Orwell's notebooks, as well as a number of personal and critical tributes to him.

"Some Letters of George Orwell," in *Encounter*, January 1962.

"George Gissing," by George Orwell in *London Magazine*, June 1960

II. OTHERS

ATKINS, JOHN: *George Orwell*. London 1954.

BRANDER, LAURENCE: *George Orwell*. London 1954.

COOK, RICHARD: "Rudyard Kipling and George Orwell," in *Modern Fiction Studies*, VII, Summer 1961.

DEUTSCHER, ISAAC: *Heretics and Renegades*. London 1953.

DUNN, AVRIL: "My Brother, George Orwell," in *Twentieth Century*, March 1961.

FYVEL, T. R.: "George Orwell and Eric Blair," in *Encounter*. July 1959.

—— and others: Pictorial feature in *Picture Post*, 8 Jan. 1955.

HOLLIS, CHRISTOPHER: *A Study of George Orwell*. London 1956.

HOPKINSON, TOM: *George Orwell*. London 1953.

HOWE, IRVING: *Politics and the Novel*. New York 1957.

LEWIS, WYNDHAM: *The Writer and the Absolute*. London 1952.

O'BRIEN, CONOR CRUISE: *Writers and Politics*. London 1965.

POTTS, PAUL: *Dante called you Beatrice*. London 1962.

PRITCHETT, V. S.: Appreciation of George Orwell in *New Statesman*. 28 Jan. 1950.

RAYMOND, JOHN: "The Barrack-Room Lawyer," in *New Statesman*, 15 Sep. 1956.

REES, RICHARD: *George Orwell—Fugitive from the Camp of Victory*. London 1961.

STRACHEY, JOHN: *The Strangled Cry*. London 1962.

SYMONS, JULIAN: "Orwell—A Reminiscence," in *London Magazine*, Sept. 1963.

TOYNBEE, PHILIP: "Orwell's Passion," in *Encounter*, August 1959.
TRILLING, LIONEL: Introduction to *Homage to Catalonia*. New York 1952.
——: "George Orwell and the Politics of Truth," in *Commentary* XIII. March 1952.
WAIN, JOHN: *Essays on Literature and Ideas*. London 1963.
WILLIAMS, RAYMOND: in *Essays in Criticism*. Oxford 1955.
WILSON, EDMUND: "Grade A Essays," in New Yorker, 13 Jan. 1951.
WOODCOCK, GEORGE: *The Crystal Spirit*. London 1967.